EvanALMIGHTY
DEVOTIONAL

Evan ALMIGHTY
DEVOTIONAL

ZONDERVAN®

ZONDERVAN.com/
AUTHORTRACKER
follow your favorite authors

invert

youth
specialties

**youth
specialties**

Evan Almighty Devotional
Copyright 2007 by Universal

Youth Specialties resources, 300 S. Pierce St., El Cajon, CA 92020 are published
by Zondervan, 5300 Patterson Ave. SE, Grand Rapids, MI 49530.

Library of Congress Cataloging-in-Publication Data

Johnson, Kevin (Kevin Walter)
  Evan Almighty devotional / Kevin Johnson and Universal Studios.
      p. cm.
  ISBN-10: 0-310-28415-5 (pbk.)
  ISBN-13: 978-0-310-28415-4 (pbk.)
  1. Christian life—Biblical teaching. 2. Devotional literature. 3. Evan
Almighty (Motion picture) I. Universal City Studios. II. Title.
  BS680.C47J63 2007
  242'.63—dc22

2007032195

Cover and interior design by David Conn

Printed in the United States of America

---

07 08 09 10 11 12 13 • 18 17 16 15 14 13 12 11 10 9 8 7 6 5 4 3 2 1

TO LYN

Because you have been crazed about doing good together since the day we met.

TABLE OF CONTENTS

CHAPTER 1

ACT JUSTLY/LOVE MERCY/WALK HUMBLY

"He has shown all you people what is good. And what does the Lord require of you? To act justly and to love mercy and to walk humbly with your God."

—*Micah 6:8*

L ook around. There's no shortage of people telling you exactly what to do—how to live your life, where to part with your time and money, how to steer clear of bad choices.

While some adults might fret about voices that entice you to do wrong, it's likely that scads of people repeatedly encourage you to do good. There are teachers who require you to volunteer and serve if you expect to pass class. Benefit concerts move you to donate to a world of worthwhile causes. Your parents no doubt set high expectations of how you should treat people when they're watching—and when they're not. Friends and peers—at least some of them, some of the time—budge you to make good decisions. And youth workers and pastors cheer you on whether you do a single, small, kind act or sign up for long, sweaty service trips.

This book is about doing all kinds of good. So what gives this message a twist that's distinct from everything else you've heard? First, it's inspired by a Universal Studios comedy, *Evan Almighty*. You might be stunned that a Hollywood blockbuster starring Steve Carell could alter your life, but this one could do exactly that.

Second, while many people point you toward doing good, they don't always explain why it's such an amazing idea. This book delivers straight-up reasons why acting for good doesn't need to be something you *have to do*. It can be something you *want to do*.

And last, this book stretches you to be kind in epic proportions. That sounds big. Bold. It is. You'll find out, however, that changing the world isn't just about giving an hour here and there or even sacrificing dozens of hours on a summer service project, as excellent as those ideas are. It's all about real, everyday actions—simple, small, kind acts, changing the world every chance you get, right where you are, right now, making a difference in the world within your reach.

GOING AROUND DOING GOOD

Humans ache to make the world a better place, even if our idea of what that entails starts and stops with padding our own nests. But maybe you have a bigger, better dream. You might want to halt global warming. To usher in world peace. To solve poverty, the AIDS crisis, slavery, or sex trafficking. You might want to ensure that people all around the globe enjoy an eternal destiny with God.

Those are awesome dreams. But for many people, they're all intention with no action. Big dreams amount to nothing more than a hazy vapor if we neglect the chance to act with love and kindness here and now.

God has dreams for you that stretch to the end of the planet and that span as long as you live and breathe. Yet his dreams for you *never* ignore right where you are, right now. God wants you living every day leaving a wake of helpfulness rather than hurt. He wants you to waft into people's lives like a fresh breeze. He packs every moment with opportunities to do good for your family, strangers seated next to you at school, and neighbors down the block and around your community.

More than a few thousand years ago the Old Testament prophet Micah wrote down God's dream for you: "He has shown all you people what is good. And what does the Lord require of you? To act justly and to love mercy and to walk humbly with your God" (Micah 6:8).

God doesn't shy away from explaining his plan for your life. Of all those voices telling you how to live, God's booms the loudest. He says he wants you to act with justice and fairness. To freely and willingly show kindness to others. To devote yourself to depending on him and going wherever he leads you.

Why bother with all that? Because love and kindness is what God does. That word for "mercy" in Micah 6:8 is *hesed*, a Hebrew term that sums up God's total love—a kindness that seeks our best even when we don't deserve it. It's a relentless, extravagant love that never stops.

It's easy to see this drive to do good in the life of Jesus. Look at Acts 10:37-38, where his close friend Peter explains what Jesus said and did all over his homeland: "You know what has happened all through the province of Judea… how

God anointed Jesus of Nazareth with the Holy Spirit and power, and how he went around doing good and healing all who were under the power of the devil, because God was with him" (TNIV). Even if you know a ton about what Jesus said and did, you might be surprised that the Bible describes a major part of his mission as "he went around doing good."

The New Testament invites you to let God's passion for doing good become your own. As the apostle Paul tells some early followers, "May our Lord Jesus Christ himself and God our Father, who loved us and by his grace gave us eternal encouragement and good hope, encourage your hearts and strengthen you in every good deed and word" (2 Thessalonians 2:16-17, TNIV).

God will never tell you to "act justly and love mercy" to earn his affection, because he already cares for you with a nonstop love. His dream is simple—that you would develop a rhythm of life where you share with others the same care he showers on you.

When you imitate God's goodness, you're engaged in authentic faith. As you pass along his care, you yourself feel more and more of God's compassion. And whenever you do an act of kindness, you make someone's life better.

You might ache to change the world. Well, God's desire to alter this planet is massive beyond all imagination. And in case you haven't caught the point, God has a place for you in his plan.

CHAPTER 2

EVAN'S PLOT/YOUR PLOT

"My food…is to do the will of him
who sent me and to finish his work."
—*John 4:34*

I f seeing a picture is worth a thousand words, then scanning a movie clip must be worth a lot more. So if you haven't yet seen *Evan Almighty*, grab a look at the trailer at www.evanalmighty.com or locate the clip elsewhere online.

In the meantime—without giving away too much of the movie's plot—here's what's happening on screen.

Flashback…

You might remember Evan Baxter (Steve Carell) as a news anchor in the movie *Bruce Almighty* (Universal Pictures 2003). The last time we saw Evan he was being tormented by rival news reporter, Bruce Nolan (Jim Carrey), live on camera from their TV station in Buffalo, New York. Very funny scene. You might note that *Bruce Almighty* has a few PG-13 elements not present in this spin-off.

Cue the start of *Evan Almighty*…

Now, elected to serve in the U.S. Congress, Evan leaves Buffalo to pursue a greater calling. But as it turns out, his ultimate duty isn't serving in the lofty ranks of America's politics. Instead he's summoned by the Almighty himself (Morgan Freeman) who hands Evan the task of constructing an ark like the boat Noah built in Old Testament times. With time ticking by and his family baffled by his newfound mission, Evan embarks on the work that God has given him.

You can't help feeling sympathy for Evan. Having campaigned on the theme of "Think Big, Think Baxter, and Change the World!" he's a guy who wants to do good by serving his country. But Evan never expects God to drop in and ask him to build a super-sized boat in his tidy, upscale neighborhood outside Washington, D.C. Just as Evan is settling into a power-filled and predictable existence, God spins him off toward an adventure of a lifetime. It's an escapade about serving humanity *way* past Evan's craziest dreams.

Got the picture? God taps Evan on the shoulder and swaps the life that Evan considers normal for something totally new.

INTERRUPTIONS OF YOUR NORMAL

You know what you expect "normal" to look like in your life. If you're like most people, your list includes shelter, food, clothes, and a car. Add in fulfilling relationships and interesting work. Top it off with health, a long life, and enough toys along the way to keep you amused and mesmerized. Maybe you even have a mental list of everything you need to feel successful…and powerful…and beautiful…and happy.

Thing is, reality is full of interruptions. Into your life slams a blindsiding situation. In a million guesses you couldn't have seen it coming, but wham—suddenly there it is. You might get propelled into a high tide of life, laughter, and love. Or tossed into low moments of anger, fear, even despair.

If you haven't experienced that firsthand in any major way, glance at your peers and adults you trust. Chances are they've experienced everything from applause, romance, wealth, and healing to hardship, broken relationships, depression, sickness, and death. Watch enough people long enough, and you'll see it all.

And yet, there's another kind of interruption.

Sometimes God breaks into your normal with a summons to launch into something new. It might be that you finally face up to one of God's clear commands. You might hear loudly that God wants to break you free from some sin that's been keeping you gagged and roped, a pattern of wrongdoing that continually hurts you and anyone nearby. Or by bringing new people, places, experiences and opportunities into your life, God might want to bust you out of the same old, same old.

God has a wild imagination. You never know what he's got coming.

ROLL WITH EVERY SURPRISE

Evan Baxter balks when God tells him to build an ark. That's the natural human reaction when our normal gets interrupted, whether we interpret what's happening as a hard knock of life or an upbeat circumstance or a nudge straight from God.

Jesus had one response to every kind of interruption during his earthly ministry. Whatever he faced, he wanted to do God's thing.

And long before Jesus walked in your world, King David penned a song that a New Testament writer would point to (Hebrews 10:5-7) and say, "That's about Jesus! That's talking about him!" David's song goes like this: "Then

I said, 'Here I am, I have come—it is written about me in the scroll. I desire to do your will, my God; your law is within my heart'" (Psalm 40:7-8).

The gist of those words is that Jesus wanted to do God's will—no matter what. Infused deep in his heart was a desire to follow God in every interruption. Jesus was ready to obey every command recorded in "the scroll," God's Scriptures, and to roll with every unexpected event. He's saying, "Here I am. Ready. Willing. Let's go."

Later we hear Jesus express that very thought. He's hanging out at a public well conversing with a shady woman, a person shunned by everyone in town. His disciples break into the conversation and say, "Rabbi—teacher—eat!" Jesus messes with them a bit, telling them he has food to eat they know nothing about. The disciples mutter and wonder who left to get lunch. Then Jesus announces, "My food...is to do the will of him who sent me and to finish his work" (John 4:34).

You can't look into your future and know how the plot of your life will play out. But whatever it brings, you can live every moment with God. You can get ready to follow him in the midst of every predictable scene and each surprise, no matter if it's a major event or a minor blip. You can commit to looking for God's path—even in the midst of the wildest interruptions.

God wants you to be prepared for him to show up in your life. He invites you to talk to him right now and tell him some simple things.

Say that you're willing to follow him even when your normal gets interrupted.

Declare that you want to be close to him no matter what.

Tell him, "Here I am. Ready. Willing. Let's go."

CHAPTER 3

IMPERFECT/BROKEN/SHATTERED

"The people living in darkness have seen a
great light; on those living in the land of the
shadow of death a light has dawned."
—*Isaiah 9:2*

There are plenty of problems in this world that could use
a bit of help—or a lot.

If your heart bleeds with even a drop of compassion,
you can't read a paper or scan online news without coming
up with a list of issues worth caring about—overwhelming
problems we dream about fixing. Like environmental
catastrophes. Conflicts and wars in the world's flashpoints.
Terrorist threats. AIDS. Homelessness. Racism. Spiritual
confusion. Religious persecution. Hunger. Slavery.

Some of these concerns hammer at you through
school and the media, so you can hardly avoid being
informed about the basics of the issues. Others slip past
your notice so that you might not hear, for example, about
riots in Estonia, or decades-long insurgencies in Sri Lanka,
or chronic government corruption in Africa that thwarts
economic development and a solution to AIDS.

At times the details get lost. You know that hunger is a problem—but you might not realize that nearly a billion people worldwide are malnourished even though the world's farmers produce enough food to feed the planet. Nearly one in three people endures disabilities or dies prematurely because of poor nutrition and outright lack of food. All four of the most common childhood illnesses—diarrhea, acute respiratory illness, malaria, and measles—are both preventable and treatable, yet poverty keeps whole communities from accessing immunizations and medicine. Therefore every day almost 16,000 children die from hunger-related sickness. Look at your watch and tick off the toll: Every five seconds, one child dies (source: bread.org).

You might assume that hunger is a far-off problem, but more than one in 10 American homes are "food-insecure," and more than four in 10 students nationwide receive free or reduced-price school lunches because of low family incomes (source: frac.org). Picture that the next time you look around your lunchroom, and don't fool yourself that some degree of lack or hunger doesn't affect people nearby. Maybe you know firsthand how it feels to go to bed with an empty stomach.

DARK WORLD

That's gut-punching news. Sadly, hunger is just one of scores of hurts. Other hurts lurk in the shadows. People live in fractured families. Countless children parent themselves, and elderly folks can feel rejected by their families and larger society. Addictions to alcohol, drugs, and gambling can trap even the most respectable of your neighbors. A significant percentage of your female and male schoolmates agonize over the secret pain of emotional, physical, and sexual abuse.

If you could peel back layers of pretending, you would see illiteracy, financial hardship, loneliness, depression, sickness, and all kinds of physical, emotional, and educational disabilities. If nothing else, almost everyone needs a boost just to get through the day.

While many of life's moments are bright and comfortable, it's no stretch to say that the world can be a tough place for any and all of us. Life is imperfect at best... frequently broken...sometimes completely shattered. And there's nothing abstract about any of this. Caught in this destruction are real people, some with faces you recognize, others with faces you overlook, the rest with faces you'll never see because they're too numerous to count. Sometimes the face scarred by hurt is the one you stare at every day in the mirror.

It's no wonder that Jesus once looked at his country's capital city and cried out, "Jerusalem, Jerusalem...how often I have longed to gather your children together, as a hen gathers her chicks under her wings, and you were not willing. Look, your house is left to you desolate" (Luke 13:34-35). He saw a world needing help—a world not always eager for his care.

LIGHT THE DARKNESS

Everywhere Jesus looked he saw desolation. Yet through his birth, life, death, and rising from the grave Jesus flat out refused to let the world stay dark and broken.

At the start of his out-in-the-open ministry, Jesus visited the place he'd been raised. In Nazareth he entered the local house of worship, as was his habit, and took a turn reading from the Scriptures. He unrolled the scroll to a spot where it says, "The Spirit of the Lord is on me, because he has anointed me to proclaim good news to the poor. He has sent me to proclaim freedom for the prisoners and recovery of sight for the blind, to set the oppressed free, to proclaim the year of the Lord's favor" (Luke 4:18-19). As every eye studied him, Jesus announced, "Today this scripture is fulfilled in your hearing" (Luke 4:21). In other words, says Jesus, "This is what I will be up to in the world."

That's bright stuff. Worldchanging stuff.

Another passage tells more about Jesus' mission. When Jesus leaves his hometown and begins to preach and act, he fulfills an Old Testament prediction: "The people living in darkness have seen a great light; on those living in the land of the shadow of death a light has dawned" (Isaiah 9:2). Jesus calls the darkness what it is. He invites people back to God and good. And he begins to call people to follow him.

OPEN YOUR EYES

You reside on a hurting planet, one burdened with problems big and small, global and close to home, obvious for all to see and hidden behind layers of pretending. True, not everything looks bleak. But there are plenty of problems in this world that could use a bit of help—or a lot.

Opening your eyes to actually see the scope and severity of these issues feels unpleasant. But recognizing the state of your world is your first step to making a difference by doing all kinds of good. Though you can study the world-sized hurts that grab headlines, there's another way to grasp the situation. All you really need to do is look hard at the people right around you. What do you see that hurts them? What problems do they struggle with day after day?

Study your world. What do you see? What do you think God would like to do about it?

CHAPTER 4

PARADISE/LOST/REMADE

"I came to give life—life in all its fullness."
—*John 10:10*

Paradise. You probably have your own vision of perfection, but try this one on for size.

There's an ocean with a tropical white-sand beach... right next to pristine mountains with chairlifts and switchback trails and high-altitude meadows and crazy wildlife that eat out of your hand...connected to a hip downtown with shopping and theatres and multiple sports venues...surrounded by tranquil countryside with four-season colors dappled with fast rivers and clear lakes. This paradise is filled with exactly the right people, who come when you beckon and depart when you want your space. You live in a mansion decorated according to your latest tastes, and in the blink of an eye you can instantly transport anywhere in all of paradise. The air is ozone-fresh and the entire environment is underscored with ever-present tunes of your choice.

That would be pleasant, no?

GOD'S PARADISE

The Bible says that at the beginning of time God designed a paradise even better than that. He created a universe where nothing existed before. He decorated the vastness of space with a sun, moon, and stars. On the third rock from one particular sun he stuck greenery in the ground, stocked the oceans, sky, and land with every variety of creatures, and crafted people as the crown of his creation. God surveyed all he had done and saw that it was "good" (Genesis 1:25). When he eyed the people he had made, he was even more pleased. Human beings, thought God, were "very good" (Genesis 1:31).

Adam and Eve completely dug each other (Genesis 2:23-25), but paradise wasn't just about a perfect environment or the first human husband and wife frolicking in a lush resort. There was also a tight relationship between God and his creation, between God and Adam and Eve. Genesis pictures God walking in the Garden of Eden (3:8), and shows God and Adam and Eve talking with each other (3:9-13).

That all sounds pleasant, does it not?

Yet you probably know the story of the world's first pair eating the forbidden fruit, taking a huge leap into sin. The account of Adam and Eve shows that they distanced themselves from God and strained their relationship with each other.

Then God bounced them from the Garden of Eden. Paradise was no more. And since that time every human being has done life just like Adam and Eve, with the same destructive results.

SCENE 3

The plot of the human story is easy to track.

Scene 1: God designs a place of blissful perfection.

Scene 2: We all mess up.

But that's not the end of the story. There's more action to play out.

Scene 3: God launches a plan to bring people back to a world even better than the one he created at the beginning of time.

That's the era where we live right now. God's plan to remake the world is in the process of unfolding. Utter perfection won't come until heaven, until God ushers us into a place that is intensely amazing, awesome beyond imagination, more satisfying than the best day of life in this world. Even better than the closing scene of *Evan Almighty*. Yet that doesn't mean we can't begin to experience his remade world right now. That's what Jesus means when he talks about freedom...sight...God's favor...good news... bright light in a dark place.

God jolted this plan into motion a long time ago. He told his Old Testament people he had a secret script for them, a story with a plot that would impact all of humankind: "'For I know the plans I have for you,' declares the Lord, 'plans to prosper you and not to harm you, plans to give you hope and a future'" (Jeremiah 29:11).

When Jesus shows up, he reads from the same script. He announces to the world, "I came to give life—life in all its fullness" (John 10:10). If you ever doubt that God is on your side—that he understands what you need not just to survive but to thrive—mull those words until you become totally convinced of his kindness toward you.

Don't take those words to mean, however, that Jesus came to wait on you like a servant. Or that his promise means his first concern is to make you as a solo individual deliriously happy. Or even that he merely wants to make you and a few friends cozy. There's far more to "life—life in all its fullness" than that. God has a whole planet he wants to remake.

You need to grab a peek at the end of God's script, because that's where you spot your place in his plan. His ultimate goal is nothing less than building an ever-expanding group of friends who belong to him—friends who honor him as their Master and rely on his care now and forever, and whose hearts beat with compassion for all the people of the world.

It's the message of 1 Peter 2:9-10: "You are a chosen people, royal priests, a holy nation, a people for God's own possession. You were chosen to tell about the wonderful acts of God, who called you out of darkness into his wonderful light. At one time you were not a people, but now you are God's people. In the past you had never received mercy, but now you have received God's mercy."

God intends that you receive mercy. And give mercy.

See, God has a dream for this world wider and more amazing than anything we can imagine. He wishes the best for every human being and for every facet of life on the planet. Human beings have trashed paradise, and God intends to repair the massive damage we've done. While he's at it, he wants to make everything even better than it was at the start.

So now you've read God's script. You know what he's up to. So when you decide to do good in the world, you're not just acting on your own. You're getting on board with God and his grand plan to remake the world.

CHAPTER 5

NOAH/FLOOD/FRESH START

"The Lord is good to everyone;
he is merciful to all he has made."
—*Psalm 145:9, NCV*

From the moment a crate of old-school tools turns up on Evan Baxter's doorstep, you know he's being called to serve as some kind of modern-day Noah. Just as he starts settling into the power-filled and predictable life of a newly-elected congressman, the guy meets someone with an entirely different plan.

God.

God says a flood is coming. God calls Evan on a mission. God interrupts Evan's normal. Makes a mess of the man's finely calculated plans.

Evan says, "This is a little conversation I like to call 'over.'"

Do you blame him?

After all, this is supposedly God Almighty showing up—in person—to ask him to do some nutzoid stuff. The Lord helps himself to a spot in the back seat of Evan's Hummer. Pops up in Evan's driveway. Causes every strain of critter to flock around Evan no matter where he goes. And he tells Evan to build an ark.

Conversation over.

STREET CRED

Evan has one main hang-up, though: He'll never get on with this God-appointed mission as long as he doubts God is credible. Believable. Trustworthy.

The same is probably true for you. You'll find it tough to commit to doing good if you don't trust the one who's calling you to act.

Of course you can surely cook up some good without God. People famous and unknown in every time and place have done superb acts with no conscious recognition of God. Theologians have said that kind of goodness is a remnant of the way God created our race—in other words, human beings can manage good from time to time because they were created in the image of a good God.

So don't think for a moment that only Christians can make this world a better place. The thing is, you're called to a way of life larger than good you can do on your own.

If you're a believer you've got the real deal sitting in the back seat of your car. The authentic Ruler of the Universe popping up in your driveway. You claim to be communicating with the God who shows up in the person of Jesus and the power of the Holy Spirit—a God who interrupts your normal and opens your eyes to every sort of need and opportunity to do good. You get to follow a divine someone who aims to make you part of his plan to change the world. And don't forget that you're supposed to get love from this God so you can give it away to others. Like 1 John 4:19 says, "We love each other as a result of his loving us first" (NLT).

If you're really going to sign up for all that, you'd better be sure that the one who's issuing all those commands isn't a toasted nutroll. Is God really so outrageously righteous that you want to dedicate your life to doing his good deeds in the world? Are his care, love, and mercy so real that you can get those things for yourself and pass them on to others?

WHO IS THIS GUY?

You'll do an Evan unless you can look at God and settle up front the question "Who is this guy?" You'll toss God a polite nod and say, "Uh. Yeah."

The Bible and even ancient historians outside the Bible offer a compelling case that Jesus actually did go around doing good. But the whole Noah episode might make you wonder about God's goodness. Nevermind scientific questions about a worldwide deluge or the modern-day expeditions combing Middle Eastern peaks to locate Noah's ark. You might worry that the God portrayed in Noah is mean and wrathful, not exactly the kind of deity qualified to lead you in a lifelong passion for doing good.

The Bible doesn't play down the fact that in the days of Noah, God is mad at humankind. Not just a man-sized miffed, but an Almighty-sized furious. He sees that people had destroyed his perfect creation—not simply the space where they live, but his plan for how they are to get along. The Bible says, "Now the Lord observed the extent of the people's wickedness, and he saw that all their thoughts were consistently and totally evil. So the Lord was sorry he had ever made them. It broke his heart" (Genesis 6:5-6, NLT). In the end God declares, "I will completely wipe out this human race that I have created" (Genesis 6:7, NLT).

There's no painless way to understand that.

We can start by trying to wrap our heads around the reality that sin had reached epic proportions. The constant and complete human-on-human evil wracked God with grief, and by his reaction we can measure his seriousness about putting an end to sin.

As we struggle to make sense of that, one fact offers hope. God purposely spares one good man along with his family and a raft of animals, then restarts the human race.

What looks like final destruction turns out to be a divine do-over for humankind, part of an optimistic plan to help creation move forward side-by-side. The Bible account says God swears to never again send a world-swamping flood, and God sets the rainbow in the sky as a sign of his promise. Subsequent human history proves that a fresh start isn't enough to solve the problem of sin, setting the stage for God's ultimate worldchanging gift, Jesus.

What we see in all of this is that a good God doesn't create human beings who have no choice but to obey him—so he gives us autonomy to pick right or wrong. A good God doesn't let evil go unchecked—if that was the case, we'd judge God as an unfair, uncaring monster. Yet a great God also doesn't give up on the world he loves—so in time he reveals the plan he's concocted to rescue and remake us.

There's nothing happy about the story of Noah—that is, unless we see it as one scene in a larger plot where God finds a way to help us do good toward him, each other, and ourselves.

The Bible declares, "The Lord is kind and shows mercy. He does not become angry quickly but is full of love. The Lord is good to everyone; he is merciful to all he has made" (Psalm 145:8-9, NCV). God is all about total love (1 John 4:7), a kindness that seeks our best even when we don't deserve it, a relentless and extravagant love that never stops (Lamentations 3:22-23). And Jesus himself is the ultimate proof of God's love for the world. Like the Bible says, "This is how we know what love is: Jesus Christ laid down his life for us" (1 John 3:16) and, "Greater love has no one than this: to lay down one's life for one's friends" (John 15:13).

If you trust that God is good, then you're way past ready to step up and take your place in his crazy plans.

CHAPTER 6

YOU/MASTERPIECE

"For we are God's masterpiece. He has created
us anew in Christ Jesus, so we can do the
good things he planned for us long ago."
—*Ephesians 2:10, NLT1996*

---

et's be realistic. If God deposited a ram and a ewe in
your back seat, you too would be yelling "SHEEP!" Like
Evan, you'd be shaken. You'd be grateful if God showed up
and explained his antics. You'd appreciate it if God made
time to look you dead in the eye and say exactly what he
expects. "You want to change the world? Me too. I want you,
Evan Baxter, to build an ark."

But let's not confuse a movie with reality. If God has
a habit of making bodily appearances to furnish you with
detailed instructions for your life, then grab a spot on a few
late-night TV shows so you can let us in on your secret of
how God guides you. If not, then you might, like Evan, have
a few reservations. Maybe you aren't totally sure that God
would actually choose *you* to be part of his plan to alter the
world for good.

Be honest. Not everyone takes you seriously. Some

teachers lump you and your classmates together as brainless bags of hormones—and do nothing more than baby-sit you until graduation. Sales clerks assume you're evil—and follow you around waiting for you to steal the store. Peers might call you hopeless—and judge, categorize, and dismiss you because of your clothes, your accessories, your hair, your music, and your friends.

If people don't always take you seriously, what makes you sure that God does? If some people think you're clueless, why dare to believe God thinks any different?

AMAZING FROM THE START

Parents melt when their babies are born. The most egotistical young man starts to gurgle cute baby noises. The most self-centered young woman gains superhuman tenacity to give birth and exist on little sleep, all to care for her precious little one. But those signs of parental adoration are nothing compared to God's great esteem for you.

King David wrote a well-known song that spells out how God sees you. Listen to David's praise-filled lyrics: "You made all the delicate, inner parts of my body and knit me together in my mother's womb. Thank you for making me so wonderfully complex! Your workmanship is marvelous— how well I know it. You watched me as I was being formed in utter seclusion, as I was woven together in the dark of the womb. You saw me before I was born. Every day of my life was recorded in your book. Every moment was laid out before a single day had passed" (Psalm 139:13-16, NLT).

God had a plan when he put you together. He made you amazingly wonderful. He supervised your assembly with tender care, watching over you long before you were born. Not only did he see you in the darkness of your mother's womb, but he foresaw every bright day that stretches out in front of you.

You might have moments when you're not thrilled about how you turned out. But God never feels that way. You might wonder how he could choose you for anything special. Yet his plans for you are stupendous.

GOD'S WORK OF ART

Actually, God has a plan for each one of us that includes good acts he has already mapped out for us. Listen to this. Ephesians 2:10 says, "For we are God's masterpiece. He has created us anew in Christ Jesus, so we can do the good things he planned for us long ago" (NLT1996).

Other words for *masterpiece* include *handiwork, workmanship,* and even *poem.* When God looks at you, he sees his own handcrafted, perfect work of art.

From the time you were little, your life has been an endless torrent of opportunities to compare yourself to your peers and a planet full of other people and know where you stack up—at the top of the heap or the bottom or somewhere in between. You might feel like nothing more than a colorful-yet-clumsy preschool fingerpainting or a misshapen junior high clay pot or tacky velvet painting hawked from the tailgate of a rusty pickup on the corner of a dirt road.

According to God, you're none of those things. Not only are you not worthless, you're a priceless masterpiece crafted by the God of the Universe. While sin has damaged God's original design for each one of us, in Christ God makes us new and keeps working in us so we look more and more like him.

WHAT NOW?

So you're special. Blah, blah, blah. You've heard it a million times.

Or have you?

The fact that you're God's masterpiece is utterly true. But it won't make a bit of difference in your life if you don't let it penetrate your mind and alter how you act. The words of Ephesians 2:10 are truer than any grade you've ever received, any end-of-the-game score, any playground taunt, any ugly name or nasty rumor spread behind your back. They mean even more than the deep love of a mom or the profound advice of a dad.

If this book had hands, it would clasp you on the shoulders, look you straight in the eyes and tell you, "You are God's masterpiece. He has created you anew in Christ Jesus, so you can do the good things he planned for you long ago." And this book wouldn't shut up until you really heard that news.

Ponder this: Within you is a unique assortment of God-given gifts, quirks, and challenges that make you a one-of-a-kind agent for change. Your talents, personality, spiritual gifts, values, and passions add up to abilities no one else has to meet needs all around you.

God doesn't make you his masterpiece just so you can help yourself to whatever you want out of life, but so you can do good things he planned even before you were born. He spotted you in the darkness of your mother's womb. He sees every bright day that stretches out before you. God doesn't think you're clueless. He's made you capable.

CHAPTER 7

NOAH AND FRIENDS/CRAZY

"Make thee an ark of gopher wood; rooms shalt
thou make in the ark, and shalt pitch it within
and without with pitch."
—*Genesis 6:14, KJV*

When God summoned Noah and told him "make thee an ark of gopher wood," the man probably had a list of questions as long as the ark he was supposed to build.

So did Evan.

Let's call this ark thing what it was—a ship or "a vessel of considerable size for deep-water navigation," saith *The American Heritage Dictionary of the English Language*. Noah's ark was 450 feet long (a football field and a half), 30 feet high (considerably taller than the bleachers next to most high school football fields), and 75 feet across (far wider than the Taco Bell, McDonald's, or mom-and-pop stand where you stop after the game). All told, Noah's ark had a deck size as big as three dozen tennis courts. Not that anyone onboard had energy for tennis after mucking out all those animal stalls.

To Noah, that job had to sound crazy. The Bible doesn't say Noah knew the tiniest bit about putting together a seaworthy vessel. It doesn't reveal that Noah lived anywhere near an ocean. So not only was God telling him to construct a gargantuan ship in his backyard, but he apparently told him to build where it was doomed to remain high and dry. While God promised that "two of every kind of bird, of every kind of animal and of every kind of creature that moves along the ground will come to you to be kept alive" (Genesis 6:20), we're not even sure if Noah had ever successfully raised a pair of hamsters much less pairs of dogs, rhinos, or orangutans.

Any sensible person could see that Noah's boat would be all decked out and stuffed to the gills with nowhere to go, and Noah had no more grounds for this crazy act than God's terse statement that he should expect a massive flood.

MORE CRAZINESS

If Noah wondered a time or two about acting on God's command, we wouldn't be surprised. And if you thumb through the pages of the Bible, you find that Noah wasn't the only person God asks to do something offbeat.

God, for example, commands Samson to never cut his hair, and the price of disobedience is that this bulked-up strongman would lose all of his physical strength. When his girlfriend snips his locks as he sleeps, Samson becomes feeble enough for his enemies to overtake him (Judges 16:17-18).

The prophet Ezekiel is called to act out God's messages to his people. God instructs the prophet to lie on his left side for 390 days, then flip to his right side for 40 additional days (Ezekiel 4:4-6).

A regal queen once perceived through her uncle's wise counsel that God had put her in a unique position to plead for the lives of the Jewish people. Esther therefore has to enter king's throne room uninvited, a crime for which she would almost surely be executed (Esther 4:12-14).

God instructs an early disciple to search out his biggest foe, a man who was arresting, torturing, and killing believers. Ananias is to pray that his enemy Paul's blindness would be healed (Acts 9:10-15).

The prophet Hosea heeds God's command to marry a prostitute who bears him three children, then leaves him. Even when Gomer deserts him, though, Hosea continues to love her (Hosea 1:2-3).

God speaks through an angel to tell Mary she would conceive and bear a son despite the fact that she's a virgin. (Luke 1:26-37).

God tells Isaiah to stroll through the streets of his nation's capital for three years—barefoot and barely clothed (Isaiah 20:2).

God speaks through a prophet to instruct Naaman to wash seven times in a dirty river in order to be cleansed of a dreaded skin disease (2 Kings 5:10-14).

Jonah gets word that he's supposed to preach to a despised neighboring people. When he flees in the opposite direction, he's swallowed by an enormous fish. After Jonah repents, the fish vomits him on shore as a sign of God's mercy (Jonah 1:1-2).

CRAZY WITH A PURPOSE

These women and men didn't always grasp the reasons for God's instructions. Many struggled with orders so seemingly unreasonable that these people had to look insane to everyone else. And if you dig into these Bible accounts, you find many of these people have blunt questions for God, just like other people then and now tapped to do his work.

Keep in mind that God's crazy-sounding commands aren't instructions to do evil stuff; and these commands were spoken to specific people, not to every follower of God—so no worries that you should feel compelled to imitate either Hosea or Isaiah. Or Mary, for that matter.

And in hindsight, none of those commands is as crazy as it first may appear. In fact, the accounts show that God always has a reason for his instructions. God's commands were never pure whim—a sort of divine "because I said so." Samson's hair, for instance, is an outward sign of his inward spiritual power. Ezekiel's flip-flopping symbolizes a total of 430 years that people had run from God. Hosea marrying a prostitute shows that while people can be unfaithful, God's love always stays strong. Isaiah's near-naked stroll warns that God's people would be conquered and led stripped into captivity. And Jonah's journey in the gut of a giant fish was the direct result of his disobedience; it's God's way to get him going in the right direction.

God asks each of these Bible giants to accomplish special tasks. Big tasks. Bizarre tasks. Trust-stretching tasks. On their way to doing good, they debate with God. Yet they obey. In the end they don't hesitate to grab their places in God's plan to change the world, even when doing what God asks seems crazy.

CHAPTER 8

YOU/CRAZY

"The orders of the Lord are right;
they make people happy."
—*Psalm 19:8, NCV*

Maybe people back in the Bible were gullible enough that God could lure them into doing some way-out deeds, but not us.

When God is about to interrupt our normal, we get a hair-raising feeling. When God wants us to do something beyond the bounds of the expected, a thought reverberates in our heads: "God must be crazy!" Like the proximity sensor on a high-end car alarm, a clear voice booms: "Back away from the embarrassment!"

That's when we feel an Evan Baxter kind of pause. "This conversation is a little thing I like to call 'over.' SHEEP!" We're not entirely sure who God is or why he wants to drag us into his plans. We quickly do the math on what obedience will cost us. We determine that doing the things God commands will no-way no-how work in our real world.

You've seen that back in the Bible God calls his people to do good. Women like Esther and Mary and men like Noah and Jonah stepped up to follow God even when it felt crazy. While their monumental feats required extra doses of faith and doggedness, their deeds aren't worlds apart from the everyday acts to which God calls you. You need the same brave trust to do what God asks.

Even so, maybe you would rather imitate Isaiah and stroll nearly naked through school than obey some of God's concrete commands about doing good—because God tells you to act in ways that don't always make sense to you or the people around you. Like these:

GOD SAYS...

"Get along."	"If it is possible, as far as it depends on you, live at peace with everyone." *(Romans 12:18)*
"Don't dis dad and mom."	"Honor your father and your mother." *(Exodus 20:12)*
"Love people who don't like you."	"I tell you, love your enemies and pray for those who persecute you." *(Matthew 5:43)*
"Help each other."	"Carry each other's burdens." *(Galatians 6:2)*
"Respect each other's bodies."	"God's will is for you to be holy, so stay away from all sexual sin." *(1 Thessalonians 4:3, NLT)*
"Be good to whomever you meet."	"As we have opportunity, let us do good to all people." *(Galatians 6:10)*

"Don't dismiss teachers or bosses or police."	"Everyone must submit to governing authorities." *(Romans 13:1, NLT)*
"Care for the planet I gave you."	"The Lord God took Adam and put him in the Garden of Eden to work it and take care of it." *(Genesis 2:15)*
"Love like I do."	"Love is patient, love is kind. It does not envy, it does not boast, it is not proud. It does not dishonor others, it is not self-seeking, it is not easily angered, it keeps no record of wrongs. Love does not delight in evil but rejoices with the truth. It always protects, always trusts, always hopes, always perseveres." *(1 Corinthians 13:4-7)*
"Don't look down on people."	"My dear brothers and sisters, how can you claim to have faith in our glorious Lord Jesus Christ if you favor some people over others?" *(James 2:1, NLT)*
"Speak kind words."	"Do not let any unwholesome talk come out of your mouths, but only what is helpful for building others up according to their needs." *(Ephesians 4:29)*

"Care for people in need."	"I was hungry and you gave me something to eat, I was thirsty and you gave me something to drink, I was a stranger and you invited me in, I needed clothes and you clothed me, I was sick and you looked after me, I was in prison and you came to visit me…. Whatever you did for one of the least of these brothers and sisters of mine, you did for me." *(Matthew 25:35-36, 40)*

While you might get plenty of people to agree that each of these are good things to do—at least in the abstract—God's commands nevertheless set off our sensors. When it comes to actually applying those words to our real-world relationships, we hear a thought echo inside: "God must be crazy!"

Every person who chooses faithfulness to God comes to a moment where his thinking about God—and God's expectations of us—undergoes a significant shift. From Ezekiel to Evan, they stop doubting God and start trusting. They quit thinking "God must be crazy!" and come to an outrageously different conclusion: "God knows what he's doing!"

If you're looking for back-up to believe that God knows what he's doing when he invites you to do good, you can find it in Psalm 19. Think on these words: "The teachings of the Lord are perfect; they give new strength. The rules of the Lord can be trusted; they make plain people wise. The orders of the Lord are right; they make people happy. The commands of the Lord are pure; they light up the way. Respect for the Lord is good; it will last forever. The judgments of the Lord are true; they are completely right" (Psalm 19:7-9, NCV).

In no way does God expect you to act stupidly. What God does ask is that you comprehend the value of all his instructions. "They are," Psalm 19 continues, "worth more than gold, even the purest gold. They are sweeter than honey, even the finest honey" (Psalm 19:10, NCV).

CHAPTER 9

SHOCKING/UNSELFISH/SERVANTHOOD

> "When you do things, do not let selfishness or pride be your guide. Instead, be humble and give more honor to others than to yourselves. Do not be interested only in your own life, but be interested in the lives of others."
> —*Philippians 2:3-4, NCV*

Jesus doesn't go to your school. Live at your house. Mix with your peers. If he did, he surely wouldn't toss you such unreasonable advice like speaking kind words, loving on enemies, and living peacefully with some of the pieces of work who sit near you on the bus.

Or would he?

You might assume that Jesus grew up in a tidy world where doing good came easy. In reality, he was a boy...a teenage guy...an adult man in a society seething with opportunities to do wrong. You don't have to read far in the Old Testament to notice that people were into enormous evil—from child sacrifice to idol worship, incest, and witchcraft. In the New Testament, life doesn't get any nicer. The apostle Paul says that people have become "filled with every kind of wickedness, evil, greed and depravity.

They are full of envy, murder, strife, deceit and malice. They are gossips, slanderers, God-haters, insolent, arrogant and boastful; they invent ways of doing evil; they disobey their parents; they have no understanding, no fidelity, no love, no mercy" (Romans 1:29-31).

Jesus didn't have some fabulous power that made him immune to temptation. In fact, he was "tempted in every way, just as we are." He was so absolutely committed to doing good that he never caved in to sin (Hebrews 4:15). In the end, people so set against who he was and what he stood for nailed him to a cross and killed him, but not until they had tortured him nearly to death.

That's far meaner than any street you live on. So rest assured Jesus knows firsthand how tough it is to do good in a bad world.

PUTTING ON THE TOWEL

Doing any kind of good can feel like a stretch, because any one of God's crazy commands can be a challenge. But get ready for more. Jesus had an even more startling instruction for his followers.

Hours before he went to the cross, Jesus led his disciples to an upstairs room. Knowing that his end was near, he wanted to make obvious the full scope of his love for them. During dinner he rose to his feet, stripped off his outer garment, and wrapped a towel around his waist. He knelt and untied the sandals of his burly, sweaty friends one by one, carefully washing the caked dirt from their feet. The act of footwashing was a practical, necessary job customarily provided for guests, but it was a task none of his disciples would dare do. The job always fell to the lowest servant of a household, and no one was about to volunteer for that role.

What Jesus did was more than a nice deed. It vividly demonstrates everything he came to do.

At the end of this scene, Jesus speaks. "Do you understand what I have done for you?" he asks. "You call me 'Teacher' and 'Lord,' and rightly so, for that is what I am." Then he gives a startling command. "Now that I, your Lord and Teacher, have washed your feet, you also should wash one another's feet. I have set you an example that you should do as I have done for you" (John 13:12-15). Got that? He's saying, "Look how I've served you. Now go and do the same."

THINK AND ACT LIKE JESUS

Paved roads, cotton socks, and anti-odor foot powder have done away with the need for frequent foot scrubbing. The wonders of modern technology, however, haven't solved a world of other problems. It's up to us to take them on, imitating Jesus by doing real acts of humble love.

The apostle Paul makes this ultra clear. Read this next passage slowly: "When you do things, do not let selfishness or pride be your guide. Instead, be humble and give more honor to others than to yourselves. Do not be interested only in your own life, but be interested in the lives of others" (Philippians 2:3-4, NCV). He goes on, "In your lives you must think and act like Christ Jesus." Then he describes how Jesus, though he is God, became a servant who obeys his Father fully, even to the point of dying on the cross (Philippians 2:5-8).

When you get right down to it, that's strange stuff. Putting aside self-centeredness. Valuing others. Watching out not just for yourself but for others as well. You could argue that such radical attitudes and actions are even weirder than building an ark.

Maybe that's true. But we can't argue that Jesus doesn't understand what it'll cost us to put on a towel like him. We fear that if we lower ourselves, people might get used to looking down on us. If we show kindness to others, we might get beaten to a pulp. If we dare to act like servants, people just might make us their slaves. Jesus knows all that. After all, he's the guy who paid the ultimate price to do the ultimate good. Like the Bible says, "When he was living as a man, he humbled himself and was fully obedient to God, even when that caused his death—death on a cross" (Philippians 2:8).

Of all the commands of God, all the ways you can do good, the call to servanthood might be the one most out of step with our culture.

UNCOMMONLY UNSELFISH

Jesus must have known we would knock our heads trying to grasp this one. Not that servanthood is so tough to understand. It's just tough to accept. Right before the guys went to the upstairs room, for example, they bicker about which of them is the greatest. Jesus has to remind them that "those who are the greatest should take the lowest rank, and the leader should be like a servant" (Luke 22:26, NLT).

What God wants is that we, like Jesus, would do things that are uncommonly unselfish. When we do, there's a promise. As Jesus wraps up this scene with his disciples, he assures them: "Now that you know these things, you will be blessed if you do them" (John 13:17).

Got that word? When you answer God's most daring calls, he will find a way to bless you.

CHAPTER 10

SMALL/NEW BIG

"Love is patient, love is kind. It does not envy,
it does not boast, it is not proud. It does not
dishonor others, it is not self-seeking, it is not
easily angered, it keeps no record of wrongs."
—*1 Corinthians 13:4-5*

Suppose that when you were a year old or so—just learning to toddle, with a darling smile dripping with drool—your parents sat you down and attempted to explain everything you would accomplish in the next 18 years. Your little brain wouldn't process much, but maybe you would get a sense of overwhelming bewilderment, at least until you went back to happily bumping around the living room.

You might get the same baffled feeling when you contemplate the largeness of changing the world. You look around and see needs that rip at your heart. You hear that God has dreams for you that stretch to the end of the planet and that span as long as you live and breathe. You discover that you are God's masterpiece, created anew in Christ Jesus so you can do the good things he planned for you long ago.

The more you learn about the crazy ways God wants you to do good, the more you decide you're up for the task.

The problem is that you could think all those fantastic thoughts and ooze all those enormous feelings yet immediately go back to bumping around the living room. You can toddle around not grasping what more is in store for you. You have no idea what next step will take you down the path of changing the world every chance you get.

THINK SMALL

It's easy to get all charged up about doing good. "If Evan Baxter can do it, so can I," or something like that. It's probably more like, "If Jesus wants me to do good, then I will." But that gush of thoughtful caring might tempt you to promise things you can't deliver. Or to attack issues too big for one person to fix. Or even to concentrate on all the giant things you want to do for God and humankind after you graduate from high school...college...medical school...get some money...win election to congress...or the presidency.

Whoa, baby.

You've already heard the value of those amazing dreams. As you look toward your next months or years, don't let go of a single one of them. But those monumental visions aren't where you start doing good. You need a now-sized view of your task.

Repeat this key phrase: "Small is the new big."

Other than Noah and Evan, God has never tapped anyone to start a do-good destiny with an ark. Actually, Genesis 6:9 says Noah had already proven himself at doing good, and Evan, for all his failings, was trying to be a decent guy. But until God tells you to draw up blueprints for an ark, think dinghy. Or inflatable raft. Or toy boat that still leaves space for you in the tub.

When you first begin to purposely, consciously engage in doing good, don't let your focus drift to the gargantuan unless it's to decide on a bite-sized piece. For now, think small. Brainstorm something you can do in the next hour or two. Or the next day or two. If you really aspire to do an act of kindness that needs a week or two or more to plan and carry out, then start mulling what smaller deeds you can do in the meantime.

THREE GUYS

Remember: Doing one small act of kindness is better than having a thousand big dreams that never get done.

In Matthew 25 Jesus unfurls a tale about three servants entrusted with safeguarding various amounts of cash when their master goes out of town. One receives a large chunk. Another gets a medium chunk. The last gets a relatively small chunk.

The first two men diligently invest the money they oversee, so that when the master returns they have each produced an ample profit. The third man, it turns out, simply buries his cash in the ground, where it fails to earn the master even a few dollars in interest. The man misses a chance to do good because he's afraid his contribution won't add up to much. He plays it safe and does nothing. In a flurry of anger, the master sets him straight.

Now, Jesus won't fly into a rage, yet he wants to educate us when we discount the small opportunities that pop up everywhere we look. He would coach us to dream of big things in the long term—but do small things in the short term. And to remember that his best dreams for us *never* ignore right where we are, right now.

You've no doubt heard the maxim "Don't sweat the small stuff." For now, God wants to tell you the opposite. He's thinking, "Don't sweat the big stuff." Instead of fretting about what you can't accomplish right now, focus on what you can do.

LOVE IS...

If you want to spot ways you can do good in small-yet-indispensable ways, pay close attention the next time you go to a wedding. Chances are good that someone will read from 1 Corinthians 13, the "Love Chapter" of the Bible. It contains great stuff to keep in mind when people get hitched, though the context of the passage has nothing to do with weddings.

It's actually about how believers should get along as they use the gifts God gives us to help each other grow. The gist of the passage is that there's nothing wrong with spectacular spiritual abilities, or having faith that can cause mountains to jump to new locations, or knowing deep things about God. Yet right at the start it warns that if we do big spiritual feats but come up short when it comes to love, we're really nothing.

Then the chapter details all the ways you can show authentic care: "Love is patient, love is kind. It does not envy, it does not boast, it is not proud. It does not dishonor others, it is not self-seeking, it is not easily angered, it keeps no record of wrongs. Love does not delight in evil but rejoices with the truth. It always protects, always trusts, always hopes, always perseveres. Love never fails" (1 Corinthians 13:4-8).

Anytime you show real love, you've done a small act that makes a big difference in someone's life. You've done real good right here, right now. And that's always the start of something big.

CHAPTER 11

POSEURS/AUTHENTIC ACTS

> "Suppose a brother or sister is without clothes
> and daily food. If one of you says to them, 'Go
> in peace; keep warm and well fed,' but does
> nothing about their physical needs, what
> good is it?"
> —*James 2:15-16*

The easiest part of changing the world is coming up with ideas. Wanting to make a difference. Having excellent intentions.

In our best human moments, we have an inner urge to do good. You can spot it when you watch a TV ad that flashes pictures of starving children, and you feel moved to give your every last cent. Or you see a little kid getting picked on, and you itch to thump the bully. Or you notice a classmate who needs help, and your heart twangs with sympathy.

Having those warm emotions can make you feel like a nice person. You might even be able to hold your own with the bevy of Miss America contestants who wish for world peace.

But doing good is about more than thinking, desiring, or wishing. It's about acting—actually accomplishing good by serving others, putting someone else before you, and committing acts of kindness, whether the good you do is blatantly in the open, totally hidden from sight, or somewhere between. When you've done good, you know it. You see a concrete result, even if the outcome isn't all you hoped it would be.

DO THE STUFF

The theme of acting on good intentions dominates the Bible.

The apostle Paul, for example, tells his young pastor friend Timothy how to talk straight to all of us who possess resources of time and energy and money. "Command them to do good," he says, "to be rich in good deeds, and to be generous and willing to share" (1 Timothy 6:18). It might seem like the more resources we have, the more we are able to do. The more important measure is how well we use whatever we have, whether it's a little or a lot.

The author of Hebrews prods us to get beyond what's comfortable so we can do good acts that feel crazy: "And do not forget to do good and to share with others, for with such sacrifices God is pleased" (Hebrews 13:16). Doing authentic good means giving of yourself, not getting by on the cheap. It's more than donating your parents' money or conning your friends into serving while you watch from the sidelines.

James informs us that passing on a chance to do good matters far more than we think. He writes, "So then, if you know the good you ought to do and don't do it, you sin" (James 4:17). You can't solve every problem in the world, but if you continually neglect chances to act, you're missing God-given opportunities. You might even be inspiring others to boldly go and do...nothing.

The Bible even says that doing good is evidence that our faith is genuine. "What good is it, my brothers and sisters, if people claim to have faith but have no deeds? Can such faith save them? Suppose a brother or sister is without clothes and daily food. If one of you says to them, 'Go in peace; keep warm and well fed,' but does nothing about their physical needs, what good is it?" (James 2:14-16).

SPIRITUAL POSEURS

That's a deep thought: Real faith demonstrates itself through real acts.

The passage from James also invites us to get honest about our responses to poverty and need.

There's yet another overarching point you don't want to miss. We need to test ourselves to see whether we're really acting for good—or just spinning our wheels thinking about it.

None of us are impressed by poseurs. We mock them because we know that simply talking big and dressing the part doesn't make anyone an authentic anything. What matters is that someone walks the talk.

That same reality check applies to doing good. It's possible to strike a concerned pose and think you've done something kind. You can feel overwhelmed by a swell of emotion and congratulate yourself as if you've accomplished something. You and your friends can work up a froth about a favorite issue. But if your concern and sensitivity and froth don't translate into action, you might be a spiritual poseur.

BUSTING A MOVE

If those thoughts make you squirm, you're normal. We're all works in progress, so our actions don't always measure up to our aspirations. There are a few things any of us can do, however, to escape the poseur trap.

You can start by recalling that small is the new big. Do good in manageable chunks, because doing one small act of kindness is better than having a thousand big dreams that never get done.

You could invite a friend to keep you accountable. Look for someone who's a little ahead of where you are—far enough along to give you tips, not so advanced that she can't relate to your struggles.

Maybe you're a too-harsh critic of yourself, and you feel incredible guilt whenever your actions don't match your drive to do good. You need to stand back, celebrate your accomplishments, and say thanks to God for the good things he's enabled you to do. Let him say to you, "Well done, good and faithful servant!" (Matthew 25:21).

If you have a hard time honestly critiquing your actions, invite God to show you how you're progressing in living up to your intentions. There's a song in Scripture that you can make your own, with words that are worth saying daily: "Search me, God, and know my heart; test me and know my anxious thoughts. See if there is any offensive way in me, and lead me in the way everlasting" (Psalm 139:23-24).

That's a prayer God will always answer. Not because God's picky or mean, but because God wants to lead you into life—life to the full.

CHAPTER 12

GOOD GOD/GOOD WORKS

"I will enjoy doing good to them."
—*Jeremiah 32:41, NCV*

Extra credit—or no extra credit? What'll it be?

You know instantly whether you're a grab-every-possible-point kind of person or a slack-in-the-back-of-the-room kind of person or someone who's content with "not bad" or "pretty good."

Maybe you're someone who's never met a piece of homework you didn't like. You constantly reach above and beyond the requirements of your toughest instructors. If a teacher doesn't offer extra credit, you invent some. If that's you, then you don't get rattled when God has a dream for you that stretches to the end of the planet and spans as long as you live. You embrace *con gusto* any long, challenging list of do-good acts. You're full of zest to do God's will right here, right now.

But if you're like the rest of us, you're not so sure you want to expend that much energy on changing the world. Put another way, what you've read so far might strike you as some sort of extra credit. Say no more, you'd maybe rather lay low and let someone else pick up the slack—or let slide altogether opportunities to do good. Lots of days, that's where lots of us live. It's nothing to be proud of, but it's the truth.

Here's the thing. Doing good isn't an optional extra. Doing it half-heartedly doesn't even make the grade. In fact, acting for good is just about the most basic, essential part of expressing your faith in Jesus that there is.

ESSENTIAL GOODS

Let's back up. When you're carving out time to read a book that focuses on doing good and why it matters, you need to hear again and again that *no good deed you can ever do will earn God's favor*. If God were tallying points on the good we do, we'd have so many botched assignments that we'd never pass the class. We're never going to wow him or win his love.

But the best news of the Bible is that because of Jesus, God doesn't track our scores. He accepts us just the way we are. We don't have to win his love—Jesus loves us even though we mess up. He's impressed with us because he created us with value and cleansed us through the cross. That's the amazing thing about what Jesus accomplished. When he died and rose he paid for all of our sins, including our apathy, lack of energy, and inaction.

Kinda sounds like it really doesn't matter if we do good.

Hold on.

That misses the point. See, right after the Bible reveals the incredible truth that we're saved by God's grace—favor we don't deserve—it bounces right into that passage you read a bit ago: "For we are God's masterpiece. He has created us anew in Christ Jesus, so we can do the good things he planned for us long ago" (Ephesians 2:10, NCV1996). Check it out for yourself.

If you're not learning to act for good, you're not giving away what you've received from God. You're missing out on what you're made for. It's like you're snoozing on the couch when you're made to leap over hurdles or run long miles on the trail. That's why doing good isn't an extra. It's an essential. It's core to who you are.

GOOD GOD

There's another reason doing good can sound optional. As Christians we get wound up about so many issues that we might overlook doing good as a key theme of the Bible. Without a fierce grip on that truth, it's tough to muster the energy to dig in to help others. We need to be fully persuaded that doing good is...really good.

Don't forget that doing good is what God is up to. Here's another verse that says it straight: "'I will make an agreement with them that will last forever. I will never turn away from them; I will always do good to them. I will make them want to respect me so they will never turn away from me. I will enjoy doing good to them'" (Jeremiah 32:40-41, NCV). Or take this one: "You are good, and what you do is good" (Psalm 119:68). Or one more: "For what you have done I will always praise you in the presence of your faithful people. And I will hope in your name, for your name is good" (Psalm 52:9). Okay, just one more you already know. Jesus "went around doing good" (Acts 10:38).

All those words about God being up to all kinds of good are signs of his *hesed*, that kindness that seeks our best even when we don't deserve it, a relentless and extravagant love that never stops. He actually enjoys doing us good.

GOOD CHILDREN

If that's what God is up to, it's no wonder that doing good isn't an optional extra for his children. It's what we're meant to be into. A good God doesn't breed bratty kids.

Look at just some of the places the Bible says this directly: "Turn from evil and do good; seek peace and pursue it" (Psalm 34:14). "Trust in the Lord and do good; dwell in the land and enjoy safe pasture" (Psalm 37:3). "I know that there is nothing better for people than to be happy and to do good while they live" (Ecclesiastes 3:12).

This call to do good is so important that we're always to keep it at the front of our minds: "Do not forget to do good and to share with others, for with such sacrifices God is pleased" (Hebrews 13:16). Doing good is the right response to people who dislike us: "Do good to those who hate you" (Luke 6:17). It's how we answer people who believe our faith is pointless: "For it is God's will that by doing good you should silence the ignorant talk of the foolish" (1 Peter 2:15). Continuing to act kindly is God's plan for us even when others treat us harshly: "So then, those who suffer according to God's will should commit themselves to their faithful Creator and continue to do good" (1 Peter 4:19). Again and again, the Bible encourages us to be persistent in doing good (see Romans 2:7, Galatians 6:9-10).

Are you convinced that doing good isn't something you should let slide?

Reading a pile of Bible verses won't by itself move us to do good. Our hearts have to be set on obeying God. Yet once we know we want to live totally devoted to God, they guide and inspire us. We can't afford to overlook the fact that doing good is central to who God is—and to the new persons God is making us to be—and to what God wants to do in the world. If doing good is something that gives God joy, then we can find ecstatic enjoyment doing good to the world around us.

CHAPTER 13

DECIDE/DO

"Do not merely listen to the word, and so
deceive yourselves. Do what it says."
—*James 1:22*

Evan has a skeptical retort to God's invitation to build an ark. "SHEEP!"

Too bad the guy didn't know what you know. Like these facts:

Doing good is at the top of God's to-do list.

When God Almighty interrupts your normal, it's an opportunity not only to respond with enthusiasm but also to live close to him.

Even though your world abounds with problems, God intends to fill it with life—life in all its fullness.

God's endless mercy makes him worth trusting.

You are God's masterpiece, perfectly crafted to do the good things he mapped out for you long ago.

Noah isn't the only human being who's received a crazy assignment from God, yet the call to servanthood might be the weirdest command of all.

Don't think that you have to start doing good by building an ark, because small is the new big.

God wants you to dream big—but do real deeds.

Doing good isn't an extra you can choose or lose. It's an essential part of who you are to be.

With that stack of reasons why doing good matters so much, you have a head start on Evan. Yet you face the same choice he faces. Are you ready to change the world—even when it seems crazy?

You can probably sort God's expectations of ways you should act for good into a couple of lists. There are deeds you believe make sense—and deeds too weird for the real world. There are people you want to help—and those you'd prefer to avoid. Or places you would be eager to do good—and others you'd rather pass up.

Those objections might shout inside your head. Yet God's call to do good isn't quiet, either. You hear it in his unambiguous Bible commands. Or from somewhere deep inside, you sense right and wrong, intuitively discerning what God wants you to do. Not only that, it's tough to ignore all the things that everyone on the planet knows are good, and we are to "be careful to do what is right in the eyes of everyone" (Romans 12:17).

So you have a choice: To build—or not to build. To start the construction project God has planned for you—or to stall him. To do good every chance you get—or to let evil prevail. There comes a time to say, "Here we go," pop open the crate of tools God has laid on your doorstep, grab a mallet, and commence pounding. In every opportunity to do good, you have a chance to say back to God not "SHEEP!" but "You want to change the world? So do I."

It's your decision.

BE A DOER

All your life you've heard slogans such as "Just Do It" and "Dare to Stay Off Drugs." But God doesn't just toss around slogans. He speaks to our minds, encourages our hearts, and wraps us in his care. And God has an even bigger, all-encompassing word that hits us right where we live: "Do not merely listen to the word, and so deceive yourselves. Do what it says" (James 1:22).

We can't claim to be doing good if we just hear God's call and do nothing about it. In fact, when we come to understand all that God has to say about doing good and yet stay unengaged, we're acting downright ridiculous. Here's how the book of James puts it: "Those who listen to the word but do not do what it says are like people who look at their faces in a mirror and, after looking at themselves, go away and immediately forget what they look like" (1:22-23).

So back to that choice. That decision you get to make. Now that you know all that you do, are you ready to tell God you want to be his agent for good in the world? Not that you've used those exact words. Or that you've gotten a badge or a shiny superhero unitard. But have you ever said something like what you heard back in the second chapter of this book, a pledge like Jesus made? He said, "Here I am. Ready. Willing. Let's go." Those aren't just words to utter once or even once in a while. It's a prayer you can breathe every moment of every day as you look for whatever God has for you to do.

You can say those words now, and say them again and again. When you do, God knows that you're eager to change the world every chance you get—even when it seems crazy.

HERE WE GO

You might agonize that if you dedicate yourself to doing good, God could leave you high and dry. You might end up like Evan, standing on the deck of a mighty ark, declaring that a flood is imminent, not seeing a drop of rain fall from the sky. You might find yourself shouting to heaven, "Is it too much to ask for a little precipitation?"

If those thoughts put you on edge, go back to what God says in his Word. Right after God tells us we're acting absurd if we gaze in a mirror and forget what we look like, he gives us this promise: "But those who look intently into the perfect law that gives freedom and continue in it—not forgetting what they have heard but doing it—they will be blessed in what they do" (James 1:25).

Whatever difficulties you face in doing good, God will equip you to deal with them. (More on that as you read on.) And rest assured that whenever you listen intently to God's commands—and act on them—God will have your back and empower your efforts.

CHAPTER 14

STAND UP/STAND ALONE

"When all our enemies heard about this, all the surrounding nations were afraid and lost their self-confidence, because they realized that this work had been done with the help of our God."
—*Nehemiah 6:16*

Any successful guy who constructs a gigantic ark in an exclusive suburban subdivision will catch insults from the neighbors. Any nose hair-shaving congressman who shows up at the Capitol looking like a werewolf will get a few howls. And any suit-wearing dad who wraps himself in a linen robe will have his family wondering if he's wandered a little too far from home.

In his attempt to change the world, Evan Baxter stands alone, mocked as "New York's Noah," "Heaven's Evan," the "Weirdo with a Beardo."

Right then no one wants to be Evan. It's a nightmare come true. Just when we get over our fears that what God wants us to do is crazy, other people notice us...stare at us... talk about us...treat us like we're out of sync with reality. Not that everyone is hostile, but sometimes the mob that gathers gets ugly. At that moment it's tempting to let others drag us into apathy, mediocrity, or out-and-out evil. If we do anything less than what God wants us to do, we've allowed ourselves to live down to people's low expectations.

There's another decision we need to make. We can choose not just to change the world when it seems crazy, but to change the world even when it means we stand alone.

NEHEMIAH

Several hundred years before Jesus lived, the people of Israel were conquered by the Persians and heaved from their land, forced to live in exile in far-off Babylon. Their sacred city of Jerusalem was leveled—temple, fortified walls, everything. Decades later a few people returned to the city and rebuilt the temple, but the stone walls of the city remained broken down.

Onto the scene pops Nehemiah (nee-uh-MY-uh), a royal servant who looks beyond his own comfort. He sees in his head what new protective walls could do. In everything he does, Nehemiah's driven to do good. When he hears about the danger faced by those few settlers in Jerusalem, he weeps (Nehemiah 1:4).

Nehemiah doesn't just hear and do nothing. He prays passionately (Nehemiah 1:4-11). He decides to do what he can to rebuild the wall. He approaches the king of Persia and receives ample help (Nehemiah 2:5-8). Nehemiah has the honored and trusted job of keeping evil people from dropping poison in the king's cup, but he leaves his cushy palace job to travel to a wasteland.

This plan to rebuild the wall of Jerusalem sounds amazing to everyone who hears it. Yet Nehemiah faces ridicule from enemies who aim to continue oppressing the people. Nehemiah reports their taunts: "When Sanballat heard that we were rebuilding the wall he exploded in anger, vilifying the Jews. In the company of his Samaritan cronies and military he let loose: 'What are these miserable Jews doing? Do they think they can get everything back to normal overnight? Make building stones out of make-believe?' At his side, Tobiah the Ammonite jumped in and said, 'That's right! What do they think they're building? Why, if a fox climbed that wall, it would fall to pieces under his weight'" (Nehemiah 4:1-3, MSG).

STONED DEAD

Nehemiah's enemies said his work was a joke. While at times you might hear a roar of applause for the good acts you do, you might get ignored. Or mocked. Or worse.

Imagine sitting on the ground completely encircled by a thick wall of people. They push up close and begin to hurl insults at you. At first their words seem ridiculous, like rocks thrown wide of their mark. Moments later a remark hits dead-on, like a boulder straight to the head. The crowd continues to hit you with stones of all sizes. Before long, you crumple into the dust in tears.

That's what sometimes happens when people try to change the world. You might face ridicule for who you are… the quality of what you do…your age…the person or people you're trying to help…the size of the task and the futility of your efforts…the "better things" you could be doing with your talents…the way you waste your time doing good.

Honestly, it's easier to fit into the world's mold than to bust out and change the world. It's easier to be unkind or even cruel than to commit an act of kindness. It's tough to embrace a challenge to do good when others don't see the point.

STANDING ALONE

You can take inventory of your own life to recall times you've experienced pressure that held you back from doing good. You know when you've dropped what you were doing and blended with the crowd. Yet you can probably also think of times when you kept doing right despite what others said.

So what kept you doing good? What secrets do you have for staying eager to be part of God's plan? How can you bottle that and keep it on hand for moments when acting for the cause of good sounds bad?

Nehemiah encounters all kinds of opposition. It starts with ridicule, when those enemies say he and his wall are a joke (Nehemiah 4:1-3). He faces distraction (6:2) when his opponents try to get him to quit his work and leave them in control. And he faces fear (6:5-6) because his enemies threaten to spread rumors that would make the king of Persia halt the work. Nehemiah fights ridicule with prayer (4:4-6). He battles against distraction with focus and determination (6:3). He squashes fear with truth (6:8).

Prayer. Focus. Determination. Truth. With those weapons and more, Nehemiah continues to build until the wall is completed. Listen to how Nehemiah describes the triumph: "When all our enemies heard about this, all the surrounding nations were afraid and lost their self-confidence, because they realized that this work had been done with the help of our God" (6:16).

There's more to the story. Though Nehemiah is the indispensable driving force behind reconstructing the wall, he doesn't build it all by himself. God wants us to change the world every chance we get—even when we stand alone. His intention, however, is that none of us ever has to go it alone for long.

CHAPTER 15

YOU AND OTHERS/DOING GOOD

"Think of ways to encourage one another
to outbursts of love and good deeds."
—*Hebrews 10:24, NLT1996*

Without Noah, the world might have come to a wet end. Without Evan, there'd be a lot of scrap lumber cluttering up a cute D.C. suburb. Without you, a bunch of good deeds planned for you long ago won't get done.

Maybe in his grand, mysterious scheme for the universe, God has a way to handle the tasks that his followers seriously botch or neglect. The Bible couldn't be clearer, however, that we, his works of art, are fundamental to his plans. When early followers of Jesus explode in loud praise for their Lord, religious impostors try to shut them up. Jesus counters that if his followers don't open their mouths in worship, "the stones will cry out" (Luke 19:40).

You don't want your prime tasks assigned to a dim-witted rock. You don't want your world to go on hurting when you have the power to intervene. Far better to step up and do all that God has for you, even if you have to stand alone from the crowd.

YOU ALONE—BUT NOT REALLY

Solo bravery is admirable. Then again, doing good all by your lonesome isn't God's intention.

Nehemiah, for example, is the key individual who drives the rebuilding of the Jerusalem wall, but he doesn't pile up tons of boulders by himself. He rallies people from the capital city and beyond to help. He assigns some to serve as builders, others as guards. The wall gets built because a whole community works together.

The church is God's way of gathering a crowd to do good, for ourselves and the whole world. It's the place where we get his mercy so we can give it to others. Each one of us is necessary in this process. Major portions of the Bible (e.g., 1 Corinthians 12-14, Ephesians 4:11-16, and Romans 12:3-8) detail how people's differing gifts mesh together to help all of us become spiritually mature and do good in our world. Each person brings a special mix of gifts—talents, personality, spiritual gifts, values, and passions. When we all do our individual parts, the church works as God intends. We grow up, and we make a difference in the world.

It's not enough to "be the body of Christ" in the abstract. Each of us is to seek out specific friends who will help us along. Like the apostle Paul tells his young pastor friend Timothy, "Flee the evil desires of youth and pursue righteousness, faith, love and peace, along with those who call on the Lord out of a pure heart" (2 Timothy 2:22). It's not much fun (or wise) to just dodge evil. There are good things you want to chase. *Righteousness* means acting properly in relationships. *Faith* isn't just a belief but a trusting commitment toward God. *Love* is unselfish concern for others. *Peace* is total well-being.

So ask yourself: Who in your immediate, everyday surroundings is helping you flee evil—and chase good?

There's one more thing. God gives us the job of keeping each other on task. Hebrews 10:24 says, "Think of ways to encourage one another to outbursts of love and good deeds" (NLT1996). The word *encourage* literally means to "irritate" or "exasperate." The goal isn't to annoy one another but to inspire and motivate each other to care intensely for other people and for our world.

Sooner or later in life we all encounter moments when we have no choice but to stand alone, but our tasks get done far better and faster if we stand together, cheering each other on as we try to change the world a bit at a time.

ARKALMIGHTY

The makers of *Evan Almighty* have created a way for you and your friends to take teamwork to the next level.

"ArkALMIGHTY" is a good deeds program that matches up the needs in a local church with the talents and skills of people in that congregation. It's a way for you to gather needs, compile them on a Web site you run, and connect needs with people who can meet them. You post your needs, and you fulfill others' needs. Really great part? It's free.

The Web site ArkALMIGHTY.com is designed to let youth groups and churches easily find ways to do practical, tangible good deeds. Can you mow a lawn? Shop for groceries? Throw a spiral? You might not equate those everyday activities with profound ways to do good, but for the people near you who can't do them, your ability and your willingness to help out is exactly what they need.

By now you know that you should be involved in doing kind acts everywhere you go. But if you're wondering why ArkALMIGHTY would encourage you to act for good within your church, it's because church is where love is supposed to start.

Imagine Christians helping fellow Christians through the tough spots of everyday life, living exactly as Jesus tells us, caring for each other. Back in that upstairs room where Jesus washes the feet of his closest followers, he says, "A new command I give you: Love one another. As I have loved you, so you must love one another" (John 13:34). He promises that something significant will result, even beyond the elderly getting their lawns mowed or the poor getting bags of groceries or the son of a single mom learning how to bullet a spiral. Jesus says, "By this everyone will know that you are my disciples, if you love one another" (John 13:35). Not by our loud T-shirts, trendy services, or posh buildings, but by our love. That's how people will see Jesus for who he really is.

By helping each other in very practical ways *in* our church, we message an extraordinary fact *out* to the world: "These people care for each other." Nothing gives us more credibility when we move beyond our church walls.

Meeting the needs within your youth group or church is just a first step. You can easily expand your reach into neighborhoods, communities, and beyond. You might set up a table at a mall and collect needs. Pay for an hour's worth of customers at a local coffee shop. Go door-to-door and serve. You'll make a dramatic difference by meeting needs big and small. Your kindness will improve lives and change the world.

CONSPIRACY OF KINDNESS

The whole idea of going about doing good isn't exactly new. Sure it's at the top of God's to-do list, and it's what Jesus is all about. But if you want to learn even more about engaging in random acts of kindness, pick up the groundbreaking book on this topic, Steve Sjogren's *Conspiracy of Kindness: A Refreshing New Approach to Sharing the Love of Jesus with Others.* More than a dozen years ago Pastor Steve's book ignited a flurry of selfless, unexpected good acts intended to help others understand God's gift of love and grace to all people. The book is still a hit.

And while you wait for that book to arrive, keep reading. You'll find out even more about how you can be unleashed to do good.

CHAPTER 16

RUN/FAST/FREE

"Let us throw off everything that hinders and the
sin that so easily entangles. And let us run with
perseverance the race marked out for us..."
—Hebrews 12:1

You may not be an Olympic hopeful for the 100-meter
sprint, but you're surely smart enough not to show up
at a race stuffed into an inflatable sumo suit. Or to take your
mark with the laces of your track shoes knotted together.

More on that in a second.

Let's back up.

Knowing the right thing to do never makes it
happen automatically. Arriving at a thoughtful, impassioned
resolution to change the world—even when it seems crazy,
or even when you stand alone—never guarantees that doing
good will be trouble-free. And just because you start out
doing good doesn't mean you have the gas to keep it up.

Most of us start with an absolutely real and powerful
intention of doing good for people near and far, but we stall
when God's call sounds crazy. Or we turn back when people

block our path. But there's another factor that keeps us from living out our intentions.

Sometimes it all just gets old. Not that we're miserable every time we try to act for good, but we have to be realistic. Doing good gets difficult.

If we want to persevere in doing good, that's a problem that needs a solution.

US—SUMO SUITS

Some of the time, our lack of energy traces right back to us.

It's like we're bending over to take our spots in the starting blocks when we realize that we can't see our shoes. We're stuffed into that sumo suit, with arms and legs jutting out with all the flexibility of pudgy wooden boards. The only move we manage is a foot-to-foot hop, and our urge to violently bounce against another sumo-suited foe overpowers any impulse to do good. And if we could see the ground beneath us, we'd glance down and realize, "I've got a problem. Major issue. My shoes are tied together."

The Bible has a word-picture of that—or something fairly close. It says, "Let us throw off everything that hinders and the sin that so easily entangles. And let us run with perseverance the race marked out for us…" (Hebrews 12:1).

Readers back in Bible days understood the running metaphor. From the original Greek Olympics to other races popular across the Roman Empire, folks knew the struggle runners faced as they pressed hard to win. They would quickly grasp the absurdity of a sumo suit. So when the author of Hebrews wants to encourage his or her readers to persevere in the Christian life, the command is "Run! Run fast and free!"

The coaching we receive is simple and effective. "Let us throw off everything that hinders." Or as *The Message* paraphrase of the Bible puts it, "Strip down, start running—and never quit!" Ancient athletes carried nothing in a race. They traveled so light that they even ran naked, refusing to let anything hold them back from victory. The point of this verse isn't to get rid of wrongdoing, because that comes in the next sentence. The coach is trying to tell us that there are many things that are just fine in and of themselves, but they hamper our wild dash. They keep us from giving our maximum efforts. And we're to ditch them.

So what does that mean?

Think of all the things that we value—the things we consider both normal and necessary for life. We want adequate money…security…to keep up the right image…to serve ourselves first…to sleep in our own bed…to do life at the right temperature… to come and go as we please…to plan ahead…to keep our options open…to be with people just like us…to avoid looking at unpleasant realities…to drive a car that might get jacked in the "wrong" neighborhood…to keep our clothes clean…to impress the opposite sex…to buy the best we can…to say what we want…to enjoy limitless fun…

The list could go on. But can you see how those good things can wrap us up like a sumo suit, preventing us from putting forth our best efforts? No matter how much we intend to do good, as long as those things keep us bound up, we will just hop on the side of the track. So our job is to strip down.

US—KNOTTED LACES

That Bible verse contains the back half of the metaphor, "the sin that so easily entangles." The message in that word picture is easier to comprehend. If getting too wrapped up in the nice things of life limits our racing ability to little hops, then messing with God's commands snarls our feet and holds us back altogether.

Maybe you're thinking of obvious sins such as murder, adultery, and stealing. True, those behaviors get in the way of doing good. But think instead of the sins more likely to trip us up. They're sins of the heart and mind, such as jealousy...bitterness...hatred...lust...rage...selfishness...arrogance...greed...sarcasm...ungratefulness. Any one of those brings our runs to a dead halt.

Until we get the situation unknotted, that is.

PRESS ON

Like you read a few chapters back, you can pray the words of Psalm 139:23-24 to ask God to show you the true you—the points where you're wrapped up with too much of something good or tangled up in sin. Say, "Search me, God, and know my heart; test me and know my anxious thoughts. See if there is any offensive way in me, and lead me in the way everlasting."

When you realize what's been holding you back, talk to God about it. If you've let something get in the way of doing good, admit it. If you've done something wrong, confess it. Like the promise of 1 John 1:8-9 says, "If we say we have no sin, we are fooling ourselves, and the truth is not in us. But if we confess our sins, he will forgive our sins, because we can trust God to do what is right. He will cleanse us from all the wrongs we have done" (NCV).

Once you've stripped down and unknotted and grabbed hold of the forgiveness that God always makes available, it's time to hear another running metaphor from the Bible, this time from the apostle Paul. Right after Paul admits that he's not a perfect person, he says, "But one thing I do: Forgetting what is behind and straining toward what is ahead, I press on toward the goal..." (Philippians 3:13-14). Even Paul messed up. But he also let God pick him up.

When you haven't lived up to your hopes and dreams of doing good, press on. You won't do anyone any good if you forfeit the race. Remind yourself that real believers aren't people who never fall down. They're people who get up and go on.

CHAPTER 17

PAIN/PAYOFF/JOY

"Let us run with perseverance the race marked
out for us, fixing our eyes on Jesus, the pioneer
and perfecter of faith. For the joy set before him
he endured the cross, scorning its shame, and sat
down at the right hand of the throne of God."

—Hebrews 12:2

Did you realize that this do-good habit isn't a sprint?

A run that requires "perseverance," after all, isn't
done in a 9.76 second flash. That kind of effort takes "drive,"
"adrenalin," maybe even "zing," but not mile-after-painful-
mile doggedness.

You catch that same point from the apostle Paul.
When he says he "presses on" and "strains" toward the
goal (Philippians 3:12-13), you get the feeling he's hit the
pavement more than once—and wheezed in a way you don't
experience when you run a few hundred yards in Phys. Ed.

Actually, you can look at 2 Corinthians 11:23-28 to
see exactly what Paul endures to carry out his mission.

He writes:

> I have worked much harder, been in prison more frequently, been flogged more severely, and been exposed to death again and again. Five times I received from the Jews the forty lashes minus one. Three times I was beaten with rods, once I was pelted with stones, three times I was shipwrecked, I spent a night and a day in the open sea, I have been constantly on the move. I have been in danger from rivers, in danger from bandits, in danger from my own people, in danger from Gentiles; in danger in the city, in danger in the country, in danger at sea; and in danger from false believers. I have labored and toiled and have often gone without sleep; I have known hunger and thirst and have often gone without food; I have been cold and naked. Besides everything else, I face daily the pressure of my concern for all the churches.

That's mindboggling. Many of the items in Paul's list have to do with various kinds of physical trauma. But don't overlook the emotional and social suffering Paul experienced, from betrayal to rejection to overwhelming distress about the welfare of believers he cared for.

WHY KEEP GOING?

Paul suffers to an extent few believers will ever experience, but his story is a real-life example of how one guy kept working to change the world—even when doing good became atrociously difficult.

But why keep going when the going gets tough?

Paul had a reason. His sufferings were anything but random. They resulted from his work as "a herald and an apostle and a teacher" of the good news about Jesus, a point he explains in 2 Timothy 1:9-12, part of a letter he wrote shortly before being executed for his faith under the Roman emperor Nero. Paul didn't keep going simply because it was the right thing to do. He lived to pass on to others the same mercy God had given him. Elsewhere he writes, "Christ Jesus came into the world to save sinners—of whom I am the worst. But for that very reason I was shown mercy so that in me, the worst of sinners, Christ Jesus might display his immense patience as an example for those who would believe in him and receive eternal life" (1 Timothy 1:15-16).

THE PAYOFF

Paul knew there was a point to his grief. His suffering would allow others to believe in Jesus and inherit life—life in all its fullness, now and forever. He saw a payoff that would make his pain worthwhile.

Jesus had the identical attitude. Check how Jesus viewed his crucifixion: "For the joy set before him he endured the cross, scorning its shame, and sat down at the right hand of the throne of God" (Hebrews 12:2). Crucifixion wasn't anything but a motherlode of joy. But Jesus foresaw what would result from his suffering and death. That phrase "scorning its shame" means he paid so little attention to the humiliation and physical pain of the cross that he didn't bother to dodge it. On the far side of the cross he saw salvation won for a world he loves. Hence his exuberant happiness.

Payoff. Results. Mission accomplished. Good done for others. God shown the honor God deserves. When doing good gets difficult, you can be sure your pain isn't in vain. Like Paul and Jesus.

You might think that these sufferings are so superhuman that you can't relate to them. But grasping how and why to persevere through rough times is part of God's plan to keep you motivated. Right after the Bible says, "Let us throw off everything that hinders and the sin that so easily entangles," it continues, "And let us run with perseverance the race marked out for us, fixing our eyes on Jesus, the pioneer and perfecter of faith. For the joy set before him he endured the cross..." (Hebrews 12:1-2).

You are to throw off the sumo suit...unknot your laces...run the race...persevere in the same way Jesus did (and Paul did) by seeing the joy on the far side of your suffering.

When you show kindness...give money...serve anyone in any way...you will only press on through all the difficulties of doing good if you're persuaded that what you're doing is your best shot at making a dent in the world's problems, changing actual lives, and helping people see God for who he really is. The conviction that what you're doing is worthwhile will give you enormous energy to keep on changing the world—even when doing good gets difficult.

Think about it: One key reason you work hard at anything in life is knowing the outcome you want to enjoy. You're willing to work really hard because you know there are results you want to reach. You choose to pay a big price in time, money, and energy because you see the benefits. It works the same way when it comes to doing good; it helps to know there's a reason to put up with discomfort.

Doing good often means you love even when you're not exactly sure what the outcome will be. And looking for a payoff that benefits others is way different than making sure you score a payback for yourself. But keep an eye on whether you're effective in doing good, because Paul was keenly aware of what he aimed to accomplish, and Jesus was sure of the results on the far side of the cross. Do good—and remind yourself that there are reasons you choose to endure.

CHAPTER 18

SAMARITAN/STUMBLE/OPPORTUNITIES

> "Love the Lord your God with all your heart and with all your soul and with all your strength and with all your mind"; and, "Love your neighbor as yourself."
> —*Luke 10:27*

Evan. The Big Kahuna. Doing his dance as he strolls into the stronghold of national political power. If he'd thought he could impact the world for good as a news anchor at a small-market TV station, he'd have stayed at home in Buffalo. Having campaigned on a promise to change the world, Evan thinks he's finally arrived in the right place to get the job done.

If you interviewed a crowd of people on the street, they might say that's exactly what it takes to really change the world. Major political power—the kind wielded by a president, senator, congressperson, or court justice. Or global fame and admiration—such as Bono. Or wealth in staggering quantities—such as Bill and Melinda Gates and their money-dispensing foundation.

ONE KIND SAMARITAN

Those people can indeed accomplish amazing acts of good. But one of the best-known stories in the Bible makes the opposite point. It's a parable about an ordinary person who bumps into an opportunity to do good.

In Luke 10 you hear the greatest commandment in the entire Bible, "'Love the Lord your God with all your heart and with all your soul and with all your strength and with all your mind'; and, 'Love your neighbor as yourself'" (Luke 10:27). Searching for a way around this challenging command, a religious expert asks Jesus, "And just how would you define 'neighbor'?" (Luke 10:29, MSG). In other words, "Whom exactly do I have to love?"

Then Jesus unfurls the story of a man beaten and stripped by thugs and left to die on the side of a road. A religious teacher walks by and sees him bleeding, but crosses over to the other side of the road and keeps walking. (Must have a sermon to preach.) Another religious leader—more of an assistant—gets a good look at the beaten man's wounds but still darts across the road. Maybe he was going to play guitar at that same worship service. Along comes a third guy—an everyday, normal person. In fact, he's a Samaritan, a despised outsider. Everyone else in the scene—and in the people listening to Jesus—sneers as soon as he mentions the man's ethnicity.

Those listeners must have flipped at the twist Jesus gives the next part: "A Samaritan traveling the road came on him. When he saw the man's condition, his heart went out to him. He gave him first aid, disinfecting and bandaging his wounds. Then he lifted him onto his donkey, led him to an inn, and made him comfortable. In the morning he took out two silver coins and gave them to the innkeeper, saying,

'Take good care of him. If it costs any more, put it on my bill—I'll pay you on my way back'" (Luke 10:33-35, MSG).

This "good Samaritan" isn't supposed to do that. Just as the Samaritan is hated by people in the crowd, the Samaritan should hate the man lying by the road. He should have been happy to see him die. But he feels deep sympathy for the man's condition, a stark contrast to the religious folks' snobby avoidance. He pours his own precious oil and wine on the man's wounds as a simple disinfectant, then gently wraps the wounds, maybe making bandages from his own garments. He heaves the dying man onto his donkey and takes him to an inn, where he cares for him. Then he pays the innkeeper the equivalent of two days' wages to watch over him, promising to pay any other bills upon his return.

As his listeners struggle to process that shocking tale, Jesus inquires, "What do you think? Which of the three became a neighbor to the man attacked by robbers?"

"The one who treated him kindly," the religious expert responds.

Then Jesus explains what it means to do good. "Go," he says, "and do the same." (Luke 10:36-37, MSG).

UNPLANNED OPPORTUNITIES

The Samaritan wasn't planning to save someone that day. He was an ordinary person who bumped into an opportunity to do good. But it's obvious that his actions flowed straight from his heart. He saw a need, and in a natural, unforced act of mercy, saved the life of someone he should have despised.

We often look up to "big people" as the real worldchangers—to people like parents, teachers, pastors, missionaries, youth workers, Christian authors and recording artists...the list goes on.

It's great to have those people on the side of good. Yet that mindset can imply that the rest of us can't make a dent in the problems of our world. It excludes all of us everyday people who can do everyday things in everyday places for other everyday people.

Here's the big question. If you're really serious about wanting to do good, where should you start?

Jesus would say "your neighbor." Who's that? People you bump into every day. Anyone you can reach out and touch right here, right now.

Shouldn't you do good toward everyone else—people in pain on the other side of the planet?

Absolutely. Never let go of your dreams to do good to people in distant places. Do your dreams as large as you can. But God also has a heart for you to help all the people in your immediate reach. It's simply not adequate to say you want to help people far away if you neglect the ones nearby.

Picture all the people you encounter in a day. Start from the time you wake up…to when you arrive at school… those peers you sit by in class and the teachers you listen to all day long…friends you meet at lunch…everyone you bump into after school in sports, clubs, work, randomly… and the people you see before you go to sleep.

Every day you stumble across people who need your help. So think of a way to change your world right here, right now. Rewind your mind to all of those people you just pictured and choose one person you know who needs what you can give.

What exactly should you do? All it takes to make that call are eyes to see, ears to hear, and a mouth to ask questions.

CHAPTER 19

WATCH/LISTEN/ASK/DO/REPEAT

"Whenever we have the opportunity,
we should do good to everyone..."
—*Galatians 6:10*

Think hard about this next question. It's not intended to be a trick, but it requires a thoughtful answer. You've heard that you are God's masterpiece. He's created you fresh in Christ Jesus so you can do the good things he planned for you long ago.

Here's the question: How exactly does God fill you in on all those good things you're supposed to do?

"The Bible" is an obvious answer. Yet many of the good deeds you can and should do aren't precisely detailed in Scripture. There are no specific words from the Almighty, for example, for not cutting places in a school lunch line. You won't flip open the Bible and find a command to put gas in the family car. You'll spend a long time searching for instructions to teach a younger sibling how to divide fractions.

Scripture is packed from front to back with excellent things to do. But God wants you not only to keep the obvious commands of the Bible but also to meet the obvious, everyday needs he puts in front of you. You can hear his all-encompassing heart in catch-all commands such as:

- "Love one another." (Spoken by Jesus in John 13:34)
- "Whenever we have the opportunity, we should do good to everyone..." (From Paul in Galatians 6:10)
- "In everything, do to others what you would have them do to you." (Jesus in Matthew 7:12)

The Bible tells you what love-in-action looks like. It illustrates many of its points through lively accounts of women and men of faith. But through those catch-all commands, the Bible coaches you to pay attention to a never-ending stream of opportunities to do good: Don't just love yourself...do good to everyone, every chance you get...always treat others the way you want to be treated.

What that means, of course, is that you can't plead ignorance when it comes to good acts you should do. You can't claim you missed the assignment or lost the instructions. You don't need to wait for God to speak to you and say, "Make thee an ark of gopher wood; rooms shalt thou make in the ark, and shalt pitch it within and without with pitch" (Genesis 6:14, KJV).

You just need to look around.

A WORLD OF NEEDY PEOPLE

Like the Samaritan who stumbles across a dying man on a roadside, you encounter God-given opportunities to do good wherever you go. Wherever you walk, there are all kinds of needy people.

You have the chance to help people who don't believe like you do—and those who do: "Whenever we have the opportunity, we should do good to everyone—especially to those in the family of faith." (Note that those words are all of Galatians 6:10, which you just read earlier.)

You have opportunities to do good to people who struggle to believe in God: "Be careful to live properly among your unbelieving neighbors. Then even if they accuse you of doing wrong, they will see your honorable behavior, and they will give honor to God when he judges the world" (1 Peter 2:12, NLT).

Don't forget your family: "Those who won't care for their relatives, especially those in their own household, have denied the true faith" (1 Timothy 5:8). A wise man named Thomas Dreier once said, "You cannot add to the peace and good will of the world if you fail to create an atmosphere of harmony and love right where you live."

None of this means you only do good to the people you like to huddle close to: Jesus said, "I say to you, love your enemies. Pray for those who hurt you...If you love only the people who love you, you will get no reward. Even the tax collectors do that. And if you are nice only to your friends, you are no better than other people. Even those who don't know God are nice to their friends" (Matthew 5:44, 46-47, NCV).

The Bible says to pay particular attention to people who have less than you do, to the oppressed, to social and economic outcasts: "Religion that God accepts as pure and without fault is this: caring for orphans or widows who need help, and keeping yourself free from the world's evil influence" (James 1:27, NCV).

Can you see it? Your world—right here, right now—overflows with people who need you.

WATCH/LISTEN/ASK/DO/REPEAT

That's a lot to keep track of. The needs even of your immediate world are enough to overwhelm any sensitive heart. But all you really need to do is mimic the Good Samaritan. Start with whatever you stumble across as you walk through life. Do what you smell right under your nose.

The process isn't rocket science. You can catch it in five words worth memorizing: **Watch/Listen/Ask/Do/Repeat.**

Start by looking around. **Watch!** What needs do you see? What bodies fill up the roadside? Of all the people you bump into each day, who most needs your help? What simple act can you do to make a difference?

You can learn a lot with your eyes, but you figure out the details with your ears. **Listen!** What hurts do you hear expressed? How do people describe a need in their own words? What do you learn by what they don't say?

When in doubt about what you can do to lend a hand, get more information. **Ask!** Don't assume you know everything. Don't barge into someone's space unless you're certain that your kind act will be welcome. Inquire whether someone would like your help.

You know the next step well. **Do!** Act on your concern. Do something with the information you gather. Make a real difference.

Once you've done all that, don't stop. **Repeat!** Keep on believing that God made you to change the world, even when it seems crazy. Even when you stand alone. Even when doing good gets difficult. God made you to change the world every chance you get.

CHAPTER 20

PRACTICAL/IDEAS

"I don't have any silver or gold for you.
But I'll give you what I have."
—*Acts 3:6, NLT*

"Changing the world" sounds like a laughably gigantic task. But when you Watch/Listen/Ask/Do/Repeat, you immediately uncover ways to do good right here, right now. Even so, what if you need some ideas to get your juices flowing?

It's intriguing to brainstorm what you could accomplish if you had a mountain of cash. But you want to aim for deeds you can actually do—and do often. Get into your head the fact that there's a world of good you can do without a lot in your pockets.

Back in the book of Acts the disciples Peter and John are walking along when a crippled beggar sticks out his hand, expecting a gift. Peter says, "I don't have any silver or gold for you. But I'll give you what I have. In the name of Jesus Christ the Nazarene, get up and walk!" (Acts 3:6, NLT). God might not give you the ability to duplicate that kind of miracle, but you still have much to offer others. Look over the following ideas:

- Have a free bake sale
- Hand out balloons to kids
- Wash windows
- Mow a yard
- Scrub toys in the church nursery
- Clean up graffiti
- Pay for the person behind you in the drive-thru
- Send a care package to troops overseas
- Stay after school and help a teacher with random tasks
- Teach an immigrant English
- Wrap a gift
- Plan an outing with someone on the fringe of your friends
- Plant flowers
- Walk a dog
- Pick up after a pet
- Have a car wash
- Listen
- Go door-to-door asking for needs (use common sense and be safe—go with friends, take an adult, and don't go out at night)
- Tutor a child struggling at school

- Help someone move
- Clean bathrooms
- Volunteer at a runaway shelter
- Paint a house or shutters
- Baby-sit for frazzled young parents
- Give out free lattes or donuts to commuters
- Organize a park, street, or vacant lot clean-up
- Do the dishes when it isn't your turn
- Collect clothing for the poor
- Buy groceries for the homebound
- Make brownies for a neighbor you don't know well
- Collect canned goods and non-perishables to stock your local food bank or soup kitchen
- Get to know someone of another race
- Bake fresh bread for your principal
- Buy a water buffalo, goat, llama or baby chicks at heifer. org
- Make room for another driver
- Speak with respect
- Teach someone to read
- Thin out your closet and give away clothes you don't regularly wear
- Set up a Web site for service agencies in your community to advertise their needs and offerings
- Spring clean a neighboring church

- Volunteer with special-needs children or adults
- Weed a garden
- Work with younger students at church
- Hand out Gatorade to joggers at a park
- Give books, videos, or DVDs you've outgrown to a worthy recipient
- Take a parking spot at the far end of the lot
- Make a deal with a gas station in a needy part of town—pay what it takes to lower gas prices for a certain number of hours
- Cook a meal
- Look your parents in their eyes and tell them you love them
- Open the door
- Give away something cool on a hot day—sodas, ice cream, popsicles
- Give away hot chocolate or coffee on a cold day
- Rake leaves
- Carry someone's groceries from the store to their car
- Do crafts with neighbor kids—or take them to a park
- Help a teacher pack up at the end of the school year
- Greet strangers
- Give an elderly neighbor a ride
- Sponsor a needy child
- Serve dinner at a shelter—bring everything for build-your-own sundaes

- Feed expired parking meters—or almost-expired meters
- Go to a Laundromat and pay for washing machines and dryers
- Volunteer working in a children's hospital unit
- Help with minor house repairs
- Smile, sing, and read books at a nursing home
- Carry out the garbage

Those ideas will work almost anywhere, anytime. You aren't limited, however, to the items on that list or even to what your own brain can think up. Get together with a friend—or a crowd of friends—and brainstorm what you can do alone and together in your homes, school, neighborhood, and community. Once you've not only come up with ideas but actually accomplished several acts of kindness right here, right now, get together again and figure out what bite-sized piece of good you can do to address a global problem.

Most of all, keep going. All the ideas you see here and generate on your own are excellent acts we can all do. In fact, they're things we know we should never stop doing. So press on. Once you're on the path of changing the world every chance you get, don't turn back.

CHAPTER 21

RECHARGE/RETHINK

"Let us not become weary in doing good, for at the proper time we will reap a harvest if we do not give up."
—*Galatians 6:9*

Although the Bible never actually states that Noah faces the same kind of heckling crowds that Evan does, it's a safe bet. Both guys presumably quit their chosen careers to build high-and-dry monstrosities. Both watch awestruck as critters wander their way to scurry onboard. Both persevere in building their boats despite a lack of cataclysmic rain. Both must have been stubborn, odd, or unbelievably godly—or some combination of the aforementioned.

Yet somewhere during all this absurdity they both must have wanted to hang up their hammers.

Somewhere during all your acting for good you too will surely feel worn out, used up, abused, doubtful of everything you're trying to accomplish. Even if others don't give you a rough time, you hear hecklers inside your skull:

- "What good will it do me to sponsor a hungry child? I can't solve world hunger."

- "Whenever I treat my siblings nicely, it just comes back to bite me."

- "Those people don't deserve me."

- "If I say one kind thing to an outcast at school, I'll never shake them."

- "I don't have time...energy...money for this."

Right about then, you need a recharge. You might even need a rethink.

RECHARGE

On down days you might feel like you're the only one in the world trying to do good. You're not. If the people in your immediate surroundings don't grasp what you're trying to accomplish, keep searching for a team who will "think of ways to encourage one another to outbursts of love and good deeds" (Hebrews 10:24, NLT1996). Lean on your youth pastor, teachers, and leading volunteers in your community. Even if you have to stand alone in acting for good, God never intends for you to go it alone for long.

You need to team with other human beings to keep you strong, but that's not the only way to recharge. You can't survive without staying connected to God, the source of all strength.

Pastor Steve Sjogren writes, "God calls us to give away what we don't have—thus we rely upon him to be the source of what is needed." Each of us is like a riverbed. God is the one spring that can keep filling us with kindness and love so we can channel that care to others.

God's love is more than a gushy emotion. You have to grasp the facts about God's unceasing love if you want to stay encouraged. A short, tight passage in the back of the New Testament contains some of the key details: Love comes from God (1 John 4:7). Our love for each other demonstrates that we know God (4:7). Our lack of love shows that we don't know God well (4:8). God proves his love by sending Jesus into the world to bring us life (4:9). Our love for God is nothing compared to the gift of Jesus coming to die for our sins (4:10). Because God loves us, we should love each other (4:11). Because God loves us, we have an endless supply of power to care (4:19).

Those are just a few of the facts that fill you in. If you get to know and experience all that the Bible tells you about God's love, you'll stay filled up.

RETHINK

On down days you might feel beat up for a reason. You might not have the whole picture on how to best help people, and in your efforts to be an awesome friend and help everyone you can you might be caving in to unreasonable demands. Don't be surprised if your well of love feels dry as dust.

The apostle Paul can help you decide if you're doing too much. He writes, "Carry each other's burdens, and in this way you will fulfill the law of Christ." Then he says something that seems contrary to his first statement. He says, "Each one shall bear his own load" (Galatians 6:5).

Paul's careful words are wise. When he says that we should help carry each other's "burdens" (6:2), he uses a word that means "heavy weight," as in, for example, rocks far too large for any one person to lift. The weight of these boulders must be shared, hoisted by a whole group. When Paul tells us to bear our own "load" (v. 6), he chooses a different word—akin to a soldier's daypack. Those are the personal responsibilities each person has to carry alone.

When doing good gets to be a burden you can't bear, for sure you need to recharge. But you might also need to rethink. The unreasonable demands of others might be putting your safety at risk or "guilting" you into doing good. You might also need to pause and scrutinize the tasks others try to put on you. While heavy burdens are meant to be shared, other loads are right-sized to carry solo. If you continually lift burdens others should handle on their own, you might be letting them shirk responsibility. If you get trapped doing the work that others should do for themselves, you're being distracted from helping people who truly need you.

DON'T GROW WEARY

Back in the Bible, faithful followers chose to obey God no matter what. Noah "did everything just as God commanded him" (Genesis 6:9). Paul ran this race "in such a way as to get the prize" (1 Corinthians 9:24). Jesus did "the will of him who sent me and to finish his work" (John 4:33-35). You can insert your name in any of those sentences. You can make that same choice to not hold anything back from God. You can choose to obey God and act for good no matter what.

When you do, God gives you a goal and a promise: "Let us not become weary in doing good, for at the proper time we will reap a harvest if we do not give up" (Galatians 6:9). Paul writes those words a few verses after he explains the difference between a "burden" and a "load." Sandwiched between those thoughts, he says that doing good is just like putting seed in the ground. Good seed will bear exquisite fruit.

That's a deep lesson, maybe difficult to accept, that you have to wait to see the results of the good you do. Any gardener, farmer, or first-grade science student can tell you that you simply don't see a harvest the day after you sow seed. When you stay true to God, however, you can be sure you will experience his blessing in "due season," in his time, way, and place.

Thinking about giving up?

Never. There's a harvest coming.

CHAPTER 22

GOD/GOOD/BOSS

"In all the work you are doing, work the best
you can. Work as if you were doing it for
the Lord, not for people. Remember that you
will receive your reward from the Lord, which
he promised to his people. You are serving
the Lord Christ."
—*Colossians 3:23-24, NCV*

You and dozens of classmates are jetting to a study expedition in the far reaches of the southern hemisphere when you crash on an uninhabited tropical island. After a few hours your teachers realize that they never signed up to chaperone a plane full of students for the remainder of their adolescence, so they march to the other side of the land mass, never to be heard from again.

You and your peers find yourselves left on your own to create a civilized society, a la *Lord of the Flies*. You need to determine the best way to survive, a fair way to split chores, and basic rules for the social order. You inadvertently stumble into a system where might makes right. When you choose a leader for your new society, everyone votes for the big senior who could single-handedly kick the whole bunch of you to the curb. While not known for his brains, he possesses obvious brawn.

BOSS GOD

Whether you know it or not, you vote to let someone rule you every day of your life.

You might think you have absolute say over yourself, but your existence doesn't work that way. Like the apostle Paul says, we're each a node on a network that includes you, God, and every other person on the planet. Actually, Paul doesn't literally use those terms, but he expresses a thought close to that when he writes, "For we do not live to ourselves alone and we do not die to ourselves alone. If we live, we live to the Lord; and if we die, we die to the Lord. So, whether we live or die, we belong to the Lord" (Romans 14:7-8). Try as you might, you can't shake your connection to God or to people. You can't camp out solo on the island.

According to the Bible, you're either on the side of good—or on team evil (Ephesians 2:2). Not only that, but people will try to run your life. If you let them, you wind up subject to the tyranny of the handful of individuals that your peers vote into power.

But God is your one rightful boss. He's the one who should get your vote. Remember? "The Lord is good to everyone; he is merciful to all he has made" (Psalm 145:9, NCV). The rest of that Old Testament hit song fills out the picture: "The Lord upholds all those who fall and lifts up all who are bowed down. The eyes of all look to you, and you give them their food at the proper time. You open your hand and satisfy the desires of every living thing. The Lord is righteous in all his ways and loving toward all he has made.

The Lord is near to all who call on him, to all who call on him in truth. He fulfills the desires of those who fear him; he hears their cry and saves them" (Psalm 145:14-19).

When God recruits you to live for him and do good, you can be sure you're working for the one who's worth trusting. It's the one voice you want to follow.

WHO RULES YOU?

When God is your boss, he's really the only one you're working for. The apostle Paul puts it like this: "In all the work you are doing, work the best you can. Work as if you were doing it for the Lord, not for people. Remember that you will receive your reward from the Lord, which he promised to his people. You are serving the Lord Christ" (Colossians 3:23-24, NCV).

What that means is this: When you work for God, you do your best all the time because you work for the best boss in the world. You do good all the time, not just when people are watching you, but only because you deeply respect God (Colossians 3:22).

When you work for God, you don't have to worry so much when people you serve treat you badly. In fact, the phrase to "work the best you can" was written to New Testament-era slaves. Realize that slavery back in Bible times wasn't what it was in the United States before the Civil War. Slaves had families, and people often sold themselves into slavery—for a time—to get ahead. Even so, if your master was harsh, punishments could be brutal, even deadly. The job of Christian slaves was to do good even when no one was watching. Why? Because their real boss could see everything from heaven. Like them, you work for one who watches over you no matter what the circumstance.

When you work for God, you also don't have to worry about impressing people with your goodness. You don't become a "do-gooder" parading your wholesome acts for the whole world to see. Jesus himself preached against this danger. Look at what he said in Matthew 6:1-4, in the hard-hitting words of *The Message* paraphrase:

> Be especially careful when you are trying to be good so that you don't make a performance out of it. It might be good theater, but the God who made you won't be applauding. When you do something for someone else, don't call attention to yourself. You've seen them in action, I'm sure—"playactors" I call them—treating prayer meeting and street corner alike as a stage, acting compassionate as long as someone is watching, playing to the crowds. They get applause, true, but that's all they get. When you help someone out, don't think about how it looks. Just do it—quietly and unobtrusively. That is the way your God, who conceived you in love, working behind the scenes, helps you out.

That passage doesn't mean you never do good in plain sight, because many of the good deeds you do will be noticed by others, either the recipient of your kindness or others watching. But if God is your boss, your motivation isn't being seen by others. Your good deeds don't become hurtful or unhealthy. You don't play to the crowd. You live for an audience of one.

So, one question…actually three: *Whom are you working for today? When you cast your vote for boss, are you letting God the Merciful control and inspire and guide your life? If not, who is running you?*

CHAPTER 23

SEIZE/NOW

"Whoever serves me must follow me;
and where I am, my servant also will be."
—*John 12:26*

I f your high school graduation ceremony is like most others, someone on stage will grab a microphone and mark that momentous occasion with words like the following: "This is your last time together as a class. You will never again be gathered together as you are today." If you graduate with seven people, that's not likely true. If you finish school with dozens or several hundred, that's dead-on accurate.

Your classmates will get jobs, head to school, move away, get hitched, breed children. They'll be busy. Some despise the high school scene and never want to look back. Others slide into destruction and don't want their old friends to see them in bad shape. A few people die far younger than anyone could imagine.

High school possesses an illusion of permanence. That's mostly all it is. An illusion.

SEIZE THE DAY

Here's a cheerful thought from King David of the Old Testament, a song he sang to God: "Lord, what are human beings that you care for them, mere mortals that you think of them? They are like a breath; their days are like a fleeting shadow" (Psalm 144:3-4).

No one likes to look at their life as "a breath," or "a fleeting shadow," or "an illusion." You expect what you do to be as rock-hard and enduring as a craggy mountain peak. You plan to make a mark, to matter, to leave the world a better place. Maybe you don't envision your name splashed in neon lights forever, but you want to live well and leave your family and friends a lasting memory of who you are and what you did.

Actually, most of us don't ever contemplate our own end and its relation to how we spend life. But there's good reason we should. It's how we see what really counts.

In the movie *Dead Poets Society,* Robin Williams plays a teacher at a prestigious prep school. One day he takes his students to a wall spread with pictures of graduates from long ago. "Move up close to the pictures," he says. "Those boys were young and intelligent and full of dreams like you. They were just like you."

Then comes the sucker punch. "They're all dead now," he continues. "They've turned to dust. But lean close—they're calling out to you. Listen! They're telling you, *'Carpe diem!' 'Seize the day!'* Can you hear them?"

It's true. Your life will pass quickly. You have to do what matters. You have to choose to do life in a way that's real and good and right.

The time to choose is now.

NO MORE STATUS QUO

The term "status quo" is defined as "the existing order of things," "current customs, practices, and power relations." Throughout this book you've heard that God isn't content with the existing order of things. He's unhappy with some of the customs, practices, and power relations that human beings have perpetuated. From long ago he planned to bring life to this planet—life in all its fullness.

God will never settle for the status quo. Chances are you don't want to, either. Yet now is the time to *carpe diem,* seize the day.

God willing, you won't be turning to dust anytime soon. Your dreams of making the world a better place, however, can easily die. When you put down this book, there's a real hazard you'll disconnect with the ideas it challenges you to apply. With each day that passes, God's call to act for good can grow fainter in your ears. And the older you get, God's voice can become still more distant. Call it a post-graduation brain rut, the frenzy of grown-up life, or whatever you want, but the sensitivity and energy you possess today for changing the world can easily fizzle tomorrow. Unless, that is, you form a consistent habit of doing acts of random kindness—now.

BE WITH JESUS

Acting for good in small ways each day might sound insignificant, a habit you can choose to glide in and out of. It's not. If you're attempting to follow a God who never settles for the status quo…who wants to breathe life into this ailing world…who is up to doing good wherever he goes…then doing good is an absolutely necessary choice to stick close to him.

Suppose you have a best friend who's completely into lacrosse. Throughout high school she's spent every free second on the field, and as she searches for the right-fit college, her leading question is always the quality of the school's team and how far she can run with her dream.

Now, if you want to stay as close as possible to that lacrosse-crazed best friend, you'll need to ponder how her love for the sport fits into your future. If you want to keep up your friendship, you'll want to share her passion for the game. You'll need to follow her to school.

On a human level that might be a stupid choice—or not. But you can't ignore the fact that God is all about one thing: Changing this world now and forever. If he spends his days wandering throughout the world doing good—and you esteem God's friendship above everything else—then you need to go with him.

Jesus says this straight-up: "Whoever serves me must follow me; and where I am, my servant also will be" (John 12:26). Not "might" follow him. Or "might be" where he is. It's "must" follow and "will be." If you want to keep up with God's passion, you need to go where he is.

The apostle Paul applauds his young pastor friend Timothy because he takes this lesson to heart. As Paul scanned all the people in his world, one stood out. Timothy cared deeply about each person he served, as deeply as Paul himself. Not just as deeply as Paul, but nonstop like God. Like Paul tells the Philippians, "I have no one else like him, who will show genuine concern for your welfare. For everyone looks out for their own interests, not those of Jesus Christ" (Philippians 2:20-21).

Like Timothy, you can be known as one who looks out for the interests of Jesus—one who goes where he goes, loves as he loves, acts for good as he acts. If you do, you will experience closeness to God others can barely begin to understand. You'll be where he is.

Before your dreams turn to dust, seize the day.

CHAPTER 24

SALT/LIGHT/SHINE

"Let your light shine before others,
that they may see your good deeds
and glorify your Father in heaven."
—Matthew 5:16

Beatle John Lennon wrote the lyric, "Imagine there's no heaven...no religion too." There's an intriguing flipside to those haunting words. Imagine if true religion invaded our lives...and we were caught up in relentless love...doing good like God asks us to. How would our world be different if we all live like the Bible teaches?

You can't help but take note of the fact that if you act in the ways God desires, you'll stand out from people around you. You'll rock your planet and make it a different place.

Jesus himself makes this clear. He tells his early followers, "You are the salt of the earth. But if the salt loses its saltiness, how can it be made salty again? It is no longer good for anything, except to be thrown out and trampled underfoot. You are the light of the world. A city on a hill cannot be hidden. Neither do people light a lamp and put it under a bowl. Instead they put it on its stand, and it gives light to everyone in the house. In the same way, let your light shine before others, that they may see your good deeds and glorify your Father in heaven" (Matthew 5:13-16).

I'M SALT?

You've probably never been compared to the substance that makes chips and almost everything else we eat taste great. The fact that your presence makes the world a more appetizing, interesting place is part of what Jesus is saying. But not all. Back in his day salt was not only employed in cooking to add flavor, it was also scattered on the ground in small amounts as a fertilizer.

More than anything else, however, salt was used as an indispensable preservative. A bit was rubbed into meat to delay spoiling. Here's the point Jesus wants to make: As salt, you keep the world from rotting.

You do that every time you stand for right in an area where the world needs a bit of help—or a lot. Instead of defaulting to the way everybody else acts, you can choose to do the good, right, kind and loving thing. When you do, there's at least a chance others will follow your lead.

The apostle Paul, for example, writes, "Do not repay anyone evil for evil" (Romans 12:13). What if you consistently heed that command?

Recall an instance where you and a friend started swapping insults. Maybe it was funny at first, but after a while you took hits in soft spots that ought not to get smacked. You felt fury, or ran away sobbing.

Suppose you had instead decided to be the one to halt the insults. Sure, you might get walloped another time or two, but for the other person, the fun of the fight would be gone. You've drawn a line between acceptable teasing and unacceptable conflict. You've preserved good. Like salt. Your saltiness could spread to your whole circle of friends and beyond.

You can apply that example to every area of life. Your quiet choices...attitudes and opinions...words...tenacious actions...everything you do can influence others to pick the same right path.

Jesus raises another point about salt, that the substance is useless if it "loses its saltiness." Technically, sodium chloride will never stop being what it is. But the methods of producing salt back in Bible times meant that impurities were always present. When impurities overpowered the real stuff, the salt was no good to anyone. It got tossed out. The lesson is that if you waffle between doing good and engaging in evil, you won't be effective. You won't impart tastiness, and you sure won't halt anyone from doing bad. Your purity is that important.

I'M LIGHT?

Maybe you've been on a night flight or atop a high hill and looked down on the stunning glow of a major city beneath you. Pinpricks of light dance in swirls of color, swaths of light and darkness.

That's pretty. But it can't quite match what Jesus is talking about. Because the buildings of entire ancient cities were often constructed of white limestone or coated with whitewash, by day they gleamed with a screaming intensity. You couldn't hide a city no matter how hard you tried. And in an era when the night sky wasn't polluted by stray electric light, even modest lamps would make a town glow bright amid the darkness.

Jesus says that you're like that lit-up city. You stand out. People spot you a long way off. That's a good thing because cities were places of relative safety compared to the dangers of thieves and bandits along roads in the countryside, or even the threat of marauding neighbors. People can come running and find shelter with you.

Like it or not, you can't escape the fact that you are light, aglow with God. Yet you do have a choice. Although God has ignited you and intends for you to burn for all to see, you can choose to hide your brightness. That's an absurd option, says Jesus. No one bothers to fire up a lamp or a torch and put it under a flame-retardant bowl. They place the lamp on a stand, where it illuminates everything around. The result of letting your light shine brightly is that people see who God is. They realize God is good. In the end, they praise him.

By the way, to be "light" is to have a real faith that *naturally* shows up where people can see it. Not long after Jesus utters these words about salt and light, he explains that people who do religion in front of others in order to be seen are nothing more than blazing hypocrites (Matthew 6:1-4).

IMAGINE

Are you ready to be salt and light?

Flip your Bible open to Matthew 5:13-16 and keep reading. These words of Jesus launch the Lord's "Sermon on the Mount," where he explains countless ways you can shine bright in a dark world. Don't miss what he says about insults and hatred (Matthew 5:21-26), sex outside of marriage (5:27-30), divorce (5:31-32), revenge (5:38-42), loving your enemies (5:43-48), generosity (6:1-4), prayer

(6:5-15, 7:7-12), worry and wanting too much stuff (6:19-34), and spiritual arrogance (6:16-18, 7:1-6).

As you ponder all those brilliant words from the Son of God—a guy who came to save the world and make it a better place now and forever—ask yourself: *Imagine how my immediate surroundings could be different if true religion invaded my life…and I was caught up in relentless love…doing good like God asks me to? What if I changed the world every chance I got?*